TIM SAWTELLE

JESUS
UNVEILED

PERSPECTIVES OF THOSE WHO ENCOUNTERED HIM

PART OF THE UNVEILED SERIES

Jesus Unveiled
Perspectives of Those Who Encountered Him – Reader's Edition
By Tim Sawtelle

Copyright © 2025 by Tim Sawtelle

ISBN: 979-8-9987097-6-0 (paperback)
ISBN: 979-8-9987097-7-7 (ebook)

Green Mountain Journey Publishing

Scripture quotations are taken from the Holy Bible, New Living Translation, copyright ©1996, 2004, 2015 by Tyndale House Foundation. Used by permission of Tyndale House Publishers, Carol Stream, Illinois 60188. All rights reserved.

Cover Design: KeithLocke.com
Edited by Sherri Sawtelle

Visit our websites at: TimSawtelle.com and GreenMountainJourney.com

Author's Note:
This book is based on the Bible, with historical and cultural background added to create a storyline that brings the events to life. Scripture references are included at the end of each chapter, and readers are encouraged to read them alongside the text. The intent is not to replace Scripture, but to help readers see the journey of Jesus—from before His birth to His ascension—through the eyes of those who were there and walked with Him.

Contents

Final Week

The Church Age
33 AD and Beyond

Dedication

Sherri

To my wife—my bride, my sweetheart. Your childlike faith and deep love for our Abba have undone me again and again through the years. The way you love Him, and the way you pour out that love to me, is overwhelming. It has inspired me, strengthened me, and spurred me on to run beside you in this life we've been blessed to share.

I am blown away at God's goodness in sharing you with me—I know it cost Him. I stand in awe of the gift God has given me in Himself and in the life I share with you. I love you more deeply than words could ever say, and I thank God every day for you.

Mom and Dad

And to my mom and dad, who are now with Jesus. You gave me the foundation of knowing that there is a God, that His Son Jesus is our Savior, and that the Bible is His Word written for us.

You lived your faith, not only in words but in action—loving so many people through the years through your sacrifices, over and over, for the sake of others. You touched lives we may never fully know until eternity. Even in the midst of your own trials, you walked with Him faithfully.

Your constant prayer for all your children was that we would "know God, love Him, and serve Him all the days of our lives." That prayer still echoes in my heart and in the hearts of my brothers and sister. It is being lived out in us with every breath we take, a testimony to the seeds of faith you planted and watered with your love and prayers.

Epigraph

From the beginning of time, God's desire has been that we would know Him—not from a distance, but personally, deeply, and truly. Every page of Scripture, every story of Jesus, reveals His heart to draw us close.

Eternal life isn't found in rituals, religion, or striving—it is found in relationship with Him.

> "And this is the way to have eternal life—to know you, the only true God, and Jesus Christ, the one you sent to earth."
>
> John 17:3, NLT

The Good News

THE JOURNEY OF KNOWING Jesus begins here. If you only knew the depth of love God has for you—you would see that He knows you, He sees you, and He invites you to turn away from the sin that weighs you down and step into the life only He can give.

> From then on Jesus began to preach, "Repent of your sins and turn to God, for the Kingdom of Heaven is near."
>
> Matthew 4:17 NLT

> "For this is how God loved the world: He gave his one and only Son, so that everyone who believes in him will not perish but have eternal life."
>
> John 3:16 NLT

> "You can enter God's Kingdom only through the narrow gate. The highway to hell is broad, and its gate

is wide for the many who choose that way. But the gateway to life is very narrow and the road is difficult, and only a few ever find it."

Matthew 7:13-14 NLT

Jesus told him, "I am the way, the truth, and the life. No one can come to the Father except through me."

John 14:6 NLT

Introduction

Jesus Unveiled is a tapestry of moments—told through the eyes of those who might have walked the dusty roads with Him, witnessed His miracles, and heard His words echo across Galilee and Judea. Though imagined from their perspectives, the truth remains the same: Jesus, the Son of God, stepped into our world and forever changed history for the glory of the Father.

As you read, let your imagination come alive. Picture the marketplace, hear the Teacher's voice, smell the dust of the roads and the bread broken at the table, taste the salt of the sea and the sweetness of new wine. Feel the moments as if you were there—standing in the crowd or kneeling at His feet.

The Bible—God's living Word—was given so that Jesus might be revealed. As the Holy Spirit opens the Scriptures, the veil is lifted and we see Him more clearly. My prayer in writing this book is that these glimpses of His story will lead you back to the the Bible, where His heart, His love, and His character are revealed.

Each chapter is rooted in the Bible passages listed at the end of each chapter. This book is not a replacement for Scripture but a companion to it—an imaginative retelling meant to stir your heart toward the living Word.

These pages can be read as a continuous story or taken slowly as devotional reflections. While not set in a perfect timeline, the chapters follow the path of my own journey to know Him more deeply. Each one is built on Scriptures God has used time and again to speak to me and to draw me nearer to Him.

I encourage you to keep your Bible open as you read; my favorite is the New Living Translation (NLT), published by Tyndale House Publishers, which makes Scripture clear and easy to understand.

May you find that these pages are only the beginning of a deeper encounter with Jesus, the living Word, who still invites us to walk with Him today.

Are you ready? Let's dive in!

The Beginning

0 - 33 AD

Zechariah

I WAS SERVING IN the temple in Jerusalem when the lot was cast in my favor. Out of all the priests that day, the honor fell to me. I was chosen to enter the sanctuary and offer incense before the Lord. My heart trembled within me, for this was no small duty. Many priests serve a lifetime and never receive such a privilege. To be chosen meant to stand before the altar of incense, carrying the prayers of Israel into the very presence of Almighty God.

When I stepped into the holy place, the air was thick with the fragrance of sacred spices. The golden lampstand flickered with gentle light, shadows stretching across the stone walls. I approached the altar, my steps careful, my heart beating fast. With trembling hands, I placed the incense on the glowing coals. The smoke rose upward, curling like living prayer, reaching toward heaven. I thought of our people outside, waiting, praying. I even thought of the prayers Elizabeth and I had lifted for years—the ones that had long seemed unanswered.

Then it happened.

The silence of the room broke. The atmosphere shifted, and I knew I was no longer alone. To the right of the altar stood a figure—radiant, holy, unlike any man I had ever seen. Fear struck me so suddenly that my knees nearly gave way. My whole body shook in terror.

The angel spoke, his voice steady and powerful: "Don't be afraid, Zechariah! God has heard your prayer. Your wife, Elizabeth, will give you a son, and you are to name him John."

The words pierced me. For years Elizabeth and I had carried the weight of barrenness. In our culture, to be childless was more than sorrow; it was shame. My beloved wife bore the pain of whispered judgments and pitying glances. And now, in our old age, the angel declared that we would have a son? My heart wrestled between joy and disbelief.

The angel spoke of more. This child would be great in the eyes of the Lord, filled with the Spirit before his birth. He would turn many hearts back to God and prepare the way for the Messiah. My thoughts spun. Could this be true? Could such a thing happen to us?

And then my lips betrayed the doubt within me. I asked, "How can I be sure this will happen? I'm an old man now, and my wife is well along in years."

The angel's eyes blazed, and his voice thundered with holy fire. "I am Gabriel! I stand in the very presence of God. It was He who sent me to bring you this good news! But since you did not believe what I said, you will be silent and unable to speak until the child is born. For my words will certainly be fulfilled at the proper time."

In that moment, my tongue failed me. My voice was gone. I tried to speak, but nothing came. Silence fell on me as heavily as the angel's words.

When I emerged from the sanctuary, the people looked at me with expectation. I tried to tell them, but no sound left my lips. My hands moved in frantic gestures and my face burned with the awe of what I had seen. They knew I had encountered a vision, though I could not explain it.

When my service ended, I returned home still mute, carrying both the weight of my unbelief and the fire of the promise. And soon, just as Gabriel had declared, Elizabeth conceived. Her joy was beyond words. For five months she kept herself in seclusion, her heart whispering, "How kind the Lord is! He has taken away my disgrace of having no children."

The months that followed were unlike any other season of my life. The silence pressed heavily on me at first. Every time I opened my mouth and no words came, I remembered the cost of my doubt. Yet in that silence, the Lord began to speak more deeply to my heart than He ever had through my voice.

I watched Elizabeth change day by day. The years of sorrow faded from her face, replaced by a glow of joy I had not seen since our youth. I longed to speak to her, to shout my love and awe at what God was doing, but I could only touch her hand, or write a few trembling words. And yet, in my quiet, I began to listen in a way I never had before. Each movement of her body, each prayer she whispered under her breath, each smile that crossed her face—it was as though the Lord Himself was teaching me to treasure the miracle He had given.

I spent hours in prayer, though no words passed my lips. My prayers were groans, thoughts, tears, silence itself—yet I knew God heard me. As Elizabeth's belly grew, so did my faith. The punishment of my silence became a gift of reflection. I thought of Abraham and Sarah, of how God had given them a son in their old age. I thought of Hannah, whose prayers for a child were answered with Samuel. And I thought of the angel's words, that my son would prepare the way for the Messiah. The Messiah! Could it be that our lives, once marked by disgrace, would now be written into the very story of God's redemption?

I could not speak, but my heart thundered every day with praise. Even in discipline, the Lord had shown mercy. And I knew, when the time came and my tongue was loosed, my first words would be worship.

Scriptures: Luke 1:5-25

Mary and Joseph

Mary's Account

I WAS SO YOUNG—BARELY more than a girl, yet already betrothed. In our culture, betrothal was binding, as sacred as marriage itself, though Joseph and I had not yet come together. The families had agreed, the bride price arranged, and soon there would be a wedding feast. I often dreamed of the life ahead, of keeping a home, grinding wheat into flour, baking bread, drawing water from the village well, and raising children. Quiet dreams of a quiet life.

That day seemed like any other in Nazareth. The streets of our village were dusty, narrow paths between stone houses. The air smelled of animals, clay ovens, and olive oil. I worked with my hands, spinning thread, humming softly to myself. Life in Galilee was hard—Romans ruled us, soldiers sometimes marched through, and the weight of taxes always hung over our families. Yet we still clung to our traditions, our festivals, our prayers, and our hope that one day Messiah would come.

Then, suddenly, light pierced the ordinary. I turned—and there he was. A figure both radiant and beautiful, unlike any man I had ever seen. His very presence made my knees weak. I could scarcely stand.

"Greetings, favored woman! The Lord is with you."

Why such words to me? I was nobody. A drumbeat of panic echoed in my ears. Fear rose in me, yet also a strange stirring, as though the air itself was alive.

He spoke again: "Don't be afraid, Mary, for you have found favor with God! You will conceive and give birth to a son, and you will name him Jesus. He will be very great, the Son of the Most High. The Lord God will give him the throne of David, and he will reign forever."

My whole body trembled. Conceive? A son? In Israel, every girl dreamed that perhaps she might be mother to Messiah—but me? How could this be? And what would people say? A betrothed woman with child before the wedding—it would be shame, disgrace, maybe worse. Families guarded honor closely, and the village tongues could be merciless.

"But how can this happen?" My voice was barely a whisper. "I am a virgin."

He answered with words I could hardly grasp: "The Holy Spirit will come upon you, and the power of the Most High will overshadow you. The child will be holy, the Son of God."

I sat in stunned silence, my mind swirling. Could this truly be God's plan? My heart fought between fear and faith. Finally, I bowed low, tears welling in my eyes. "I am the Lord's servant. May everything you have said come true."

When he left, the silence seemed louder than before. I touched my stomach, flat and ordinary, yet I knew heaven had touched earth. And I knew my life—and the world—would never be the same.

Joseph's Account

Nazareth was my home, a place where everyone knew everyone. I worked with wood and stone, laboring with my hands to prepare for a household of my own. As a man of Israel, honor was everything. We lived under Roman rule, taxed and pressed, but we clung fiercely to our faith and the hope of Messiah. My betrothal to Mary was a joy—I was building for our future, saving for the wedding feast, dreaming of children to carry on the line of David.

Then the news came. Mary was with child.

When I first heard it, I was left stunned. My stomach churned, and I felt as though the ground itself had slipped away. She told me an angel had spoken to her, that this child was from the Spirit of God. I wanted to believe her—oh, how I wanted to—but it was more than my mind could take in.

Honor. Law. Mercy. These words warred inside me. If I exposed her publicly, the elders could condemn her. In our Law, betrothal was covenant—her pregnancy would be seen as betrayal. Yet my heart burned at the thought of her shame, her life endangered.

I lay awake at night, staring at the beams of my roof, the scent of wood smoke in the air. My calloused hands pressed against my face as I wrestled. What should I do? I resolved, with great sorrow, to divorce her quietly. To end the betrothal without spectacle, hoping to shield her from the worst.

That night, sleep finally came, heavy and restless. And then—light in my dream. An angel of the Lord stood before me. His voice was strong, yet steady: "Joseph, son of David, do not be afraid to take Mary as your wife. The child within her was conceived by the Holy Spirit. She will bear a son, and you are to name him Jesus, for he will save his people from their sins."

I awoke with my heart pounding, the echo of those words burning in me. The air from my workshop next door smelled of fresh shavings, but I could hardly see for the tears in my eyes. Son of David—that was me, carrying the royal line. And this child—this Jesus—would be Savior.

There was no more doubt nor fear. I rose with the dawn, the sky just beginning to glow over the hills of Galilee. My path was clear. I would obey. I would take Mary as my wife. Her shame was no shame—it was the holy plan of God.

When I saw her again, her eyes searching mine, I spoke softly, yet with conviction: "Mary, I believe."

Scriptures: Luke 1:26-38 & Matthew 1:18-24

Elizabeth

WHEN I LOOK BACK on those days, my heart still trembles with awe. As a daughter of Aaron's line, I had carried both joy and sorrow through many years. My husband Zechariah was a priest—faithful, blameless, devoted to the service of the Lord. Yet we bore the sorrow of barrenness. In our culture, children were seen as a heritage from the Lord, a sign of His blessing. To be childless was often thought to mean God's displeasure. Though we served Him, though we prayed, we lived with silence in our home and whispers in our village.

But then, in my old age, God remembered me. My womb, once closed, now carried life. Each morning as I rose, I pressed my hand against the swelling of my belly, hardly believing it. I remembered the words of the prophet Malachi: "Look, I am sending you the prophet Elijah before the great and dreadful day of the Lord arrives" (Malachi 4:5 NLT). Could my son be part of this promise? Could it be that my disgrace was being turned into a story of redemption?

It was then that Mary, my young cousin, came to me. She had traveled from Nazareth to the hill country of Judea, weary from the road yet radiant with purpose. The moment I heard her greeting, something sacred happened. My child leapt within me—not just a simple kick, but as though he himself recognized the One she carried. In that instant, the Holy Spirit filled me, and I cried out, "God has blessed you above all women, and your child is blessed. Why am I so honored, that the mother of my Lord should visit me?".

I knew then: Mary bore the Messiah. The ancient promises spoken in our synagogues since childhood—Isaiah's virgin birth, Micah's ruler from Bethlehem—all of it was alive in her womb. She answered my cry with a song that still lingers in my ears:
"Oh, how my soul praises the Lord. How my spirit rejoices in God my Savior!".

For three months she remained with me. We prayed together, broke bread together, whispered of the mysteries forming within us. I can still smell the bread baking, hear her laughter filling my quiet home, feel her hand gripping mine as we marveled at the promises of God.

At last, my labor began, and the women of the village gathered close. The warm scent of oil lamps mingled with the shuffle of sandals and gentle words of encouragement. Then—his cry rose above it all. My John. The name the angel had spoken: 'The Lord is gracious.' And in that moment, I knew how true it was.

On the eighth day, as our custom commanded, we brought him to be circumcised. The courtyard swelled with neighbors and family, buzzing with expectation. They pressed me, "Name him after his father." But I knew what God had said. I shook my head and declared, "No. His name is John." Shock rippled through them. "But no one in your family is called that!"

They turned to Zechariah, still mute from his encounter in the Temple. He took his tablet and wrote firmly: "His name is John." In that moment his tongue was loosed, and his voice thundered with praise to God.

And then came the words I will never forget. The Spirit filled him, and he prophesied over both Messiah and our son:
"And you, my little son, will be called the prophet of the Most High, because you will prepare the way for the Lord. You will tell his people how to find salvation through forgiveness of their sins".

Tears streamed down my face as I held my baby close. His tiny fists clenched, his eyes bright and searching, and yet over him hung a calling greater than kings. He was not just my miracle—he was God's messenger. A voice destined to cry out in the wilderness, preparing hearts for the Savior.

As John grew, I could see that he was not like other children. While others crowded in the marketplace chasing one another in play, my son often wandered to the edges of the hills, staring out at the horizon as though waiting for someone unseen. He loved the wild places. The desert winds did not scare him but seemed to call to him. I would watch him climb the rocky paths, his tunic dust-stained, his hair tangled by the breeze, his laughter carried by the wind. There was a fierceness in him, but also a gentleness. When he was still small, he would come and lay his head against me, asking me again about the story of his birth, of the angel who had spoken to his father, of the leap he made inside my womb when Mary entered the room.

At night, when all was quiet, I prayed over him. I asked the Lord to give him courage for the wilderness, strength for the message, and humility to always know that he was only the forerunner, not the Light itself.

Though I knew he was set apart, I was still his mother. I kissed his scraped knees, I taught him the Psalms, I told him of the great prophets Elijah and Isaiah. I reminded him always that "the Lord is gracious," for that was his name.

And deep in my heart, I knew there would come a day when I would have to let him go into the wild fully, to take up his voice and cry out to Israel: "Prepare the way for the Lord!" Until then, I treasured every moment—his laughter, his questions, his steady gaze toward heaven.

The Lord had taken my barrenness and turned it into abundance. He had lifted my shame and replaced it with joy. My son John—my gift, my prophet, my joy. And through him, the way was being prepared for the Lord Himself.

Scriptures: Luke 1:39-80

Shepherds

THAT NIGHT CHANGED EVERYTHING. For though shepherds had watched these hills for generations, nothing could prepare us for what we saw.

We were the lowest of men in those days. Shepherds were considered unclean, too rough to be welcome in the courts of the temple, too poor to matter in the eyes of Rome. The religious leaders in Jerusalem often passed us by with disgust. Yet we knew the Scriptures as best as we could, stories passed down from our fathers and grandfathers around fires just like ours. The promise of the Messiah was the hope of every generation—the One who would come from David's line, who would deliver us from oppression, who would bring peace and reign forever.

The beautiful night sky was deep and quiet. The smell of smoke clung to my clothes. The sheep shuffled close, their woolly warmth a comfort against the chill. My hands were rough, my body tired from long days and longer nights. I thought it would be another night of keeping watch, protecting the flock from wolves or thieves.

Then—light! Blinding, brilliant, pure light that turned night into day. My heart seized, a gasp escaped me, and we all fell to the ground. My ears rang, my body shook, and my thoughts raced. Was this judgment? Was this the end of the world?

Then a voice—clear, strong, but filled with peace—broke through the terror. "Don't be afraid! I bring you good news that will bring great joy to all people. The Savior—yes, the Messiah, the Lord—has been born today in Bethlehem, the city of David!"

Born. Today. In Bethlehem!

I could hardly grasp the words. For generations we had prayed, wept, and longed for deliverance. Our fathers had died under Roman rule waiting for Him. Our mothers had whispered the promises of the prophets to us as children. Could it be? After hundreds of years of silence, after centuries of waiting—this very night, the Messiah was born?

I remember thinking, Why us? Why here? Why shepherds? Why would the Holy One of Israel send His heavenly messenger to men like us—the least, the forgotten, the poor? And yet in that moment I felt it: He was not ashamed of us. Heaven's glory came down to our lowly field, as if to say, This news is for you first—for those who thought they had no place at the table, for the humble, for the broken.

And then, before my heart could steady, the sky erupted. Angels—thousands upon thousands of them—filling the heavens with a glory I had no words for. The night was swallowed in light so pure, so radiant, that it seemed the stars themselves bowed before it. Their voices rose together, countless yet perfectly united, rolling over the hills like waves of thunder and yet carrying the sweetness of a hundred harps. There were tones I had never heard before on this earth, sounds that seemed to pierce straight through flesh and bone and settle deep into the soul. Some carried the power of trumpets, others the resonance of mighty horns, all blending in harmony that shook the air around us. My whole body trembled as tears blurred my eyes, for I was hearing heaven's song—the very courts of God spilling into our world. "Glory to God in highest heaven, and peace on earth to those with whom God is pleased." The earth beneath us quaked as if joining their praise, the dust rising from where we had fallen, the sheep bleating in terror, yet all of creation seemed caught in awe. None of it mattered but this: Heaven was touching earth. God Himself was speaking to us.

When the sky grew still again, silence seemed deafening. We stared at each other with wide eyes, our hearts pounding with both fear and joy. And we knew—without a single doubt—we had to go. We had to see. If the Messiah had truly come, nothing else in the world mattered.

We ran down those rocky paths, the sharp stones cutting into our sandals, our cloaks flapping behind us. My thoughts burned with awe: The Messiah is here. Today. In my lifetime. In my town. In my sight. And somehow... God chose me to hear it first.

When we found Him, just as the angel had said—a baby wrapped in cloth, lying in a manger—I could barely breathe. The smell of hay, the warm breath of animals, the quiet cooing of the

Child... it was so ordinary. And yet this ordinary sight held the extraordinary truth: here was the One our people had waited for since the days of Abraham, Isaac, and Jacob.

I fell to my knees, the rough straw biting into my skin, and whispered what I could barely speak: "Messiah. Lord. Savior."

We left the stable and could not keep our excitement to ourselves. Every street, every passerby in Bethlehem heard our voices that night. We proclaimed what we had seen, and though many doubted, many more marveled. Some scoffed, but others clutched their children close, tears of hope rising in their eyes.

We returned back to our fields, but we were never the same. Every breath, every step was filled with praise: "Glory to God in highest heaven, and peace on earth to those with whom God is pleased."

Scriptures: Luke 2:1-20

Simeon and Anna

Mary's account:

THE TEMPLE COURTS were crowded that morning—families with infants, men leading lambs and doves for sacrifice, priests moving quickly through their duties. The sound of chanting psalms echoed through marble arches, blending with the murmur of voices and the cries of children. The smell of incense drifted from the inner courts, mingling with the sharp scent of animal hides and straw.

In that swirl of humanity, Simeon approached. His white beard trembled as he walked, his staff tapping against the stone pavement. People made way for him—perhaps they knew him as a righteous man, perhaps they simply sensed the weight of God's Spirit upon him. When his eyes locked onto Jesus, it was as though time itself slowed.

He stretched out his arms, and without hesitation, I placed Jesus into his embrace. The noise of the court seemed to hush around us as Simeon lifted his voice:

"Sovereign Lord, now let Your servant die in peace, as You have promised. I have seen Your salvation, which You have prepared for all people. He is a light to reveal God to the nations, and He is the glory of Your people Israel."

The words carried across the court, silencing those who heard them. Mothers turned their heads, priests paused in mid-step, and even the doves in their cages seemed to still. His words pierced my soul. He was declaring openly, before all, who Jesus was—the salvation of God, not just for us, but for all nations.

Then Simeon turned his gaze on me. His eyes were kind, yet carried sorrow. "This Child is destined to cause many in Israel to fall, and many others to rise. He has been sent as a sign from God, but many will oppose Him. As a result, the deepest thoughts of many hearts will be revealed. And a sword will pierce your very soul."

His words cut into me more deeply than I could bear. My arms longed to take Jesus back, to shield Him from such a destiny. Yet even as tears filled my eyes, I knew this was God's plan, not mine to change. Around me, whispers began to rise—people questioning, others marveling. Some shook their heads in doubt, others looked on with hope.

Joseph's account:

As Simeon handed Jesus back to Mary, I felt the weight of his words press on me. I wanted to protest, to say that my son would not be opposed, that no sword would pierce Mary's heart. But I knew this was His destiny.

Then she came—Anna. Her face was weathered by years, her back slightly bent, yet her steps were filled with strength born of devotion. I had seen her before in the temple, always praying, always fasting. Some said she had lived here most of her life, a widow who gave herself fully to the Lord.

When she saw Jesus, her face lit up with a fire that drew every eye around her. She lifted her hands toward heaven, her voice crying out: "Praise be to the Lord! This is the One! The redemption of Jerusalem has come!"

Her words stirred the court like a gust of wind. Pilgrims dropped what they were carrying to listen. A young Levite paused mid-song, staring in wonder. A priest turned sharply, his brows furrowed, as if to silence her—but her joy could not be contained. She turned to those gathered, speaking of Jesus to anyone who would listen: "He is the salvation of our people! The promise we have waited for!"

The crowd pressed closer, some with awe in their eyes, some with skepticism. A mother beside us clutched her own infant tighter, staring at Jesus as though trying to see what Anna saw. A group of men exchanged whispers—some nodding, others frowning.

I stood in the center of it all, my hand on Mary's shoulder, watching heaven's message ripple across the temple courts through Simeon and Anna. What began with the quiet circumcision and the naming of our Son, now burst openly into public declaration.

Mary's account:

I could feel the weight of every eye upon us. My cheeks were wet with tears, my arms tight around Jesus. It was as though God

Himself had chosen this moment, this place, these voices, to reveal His promise. Simeon with his steady, Spirit-led prophecy. Anna with her uncontainable joy.

The temple courts, filled with noise and busyness just moments before, had become the stage for heaven's announcement. The name we had spoken over Him—Jesus, Salvation—was now being proclaimed by others, confirmed by witnesses who had waited their whole lives for this moment.

We left the temple in silence, but I knew the ripples of that day would not fade. People had heard. Some believed, some doubted, but none could deny that something holy had happened.

I pressed my cheek against His head and whispered, "You are God's promise. You are His salvation. May I be faithful with all God has entrusted to me."

Scriptures: Luke 2:21-40

Three Kings

FOR GENERATIONS, WE STUDIED the heavens. Among our people we were called magi—scholars, priests, seekers of mysteries. We pored over the writings of our ancestors, scrolls carried through Babylon, Persia, and lands far beyond.

Some of those scrolls contained the words of the Hebrew prophet Daniel, who had foretold of a King whose dominion would never end. And so, with eyes to the sky and hearts waiting, we searched.

Night after night we watched. Then one evening, as desert winds whispered across the sands and the stars traced their familiar paths, a light broke forth. A star unlike any other—steady, brilliant, and alive with a glory we could not explain. It was not the kind of star that passes quickly; it was a sign. We knew. The King had come.

To leave our homeland was no light decision. Yet how could we stay? We packed what we could, gathered treasures worthy of a king, and joined caravans across the wilderness. The days scorched our skin; the nights pierced our bones with cold. Sandstorms blinded us, rivers chilled us, mountains stretched endlessly.

Markets shouted with the voices of merchants; camels groaned beneath their burdens; spices and smoke drifted through the air of every city we passed. But still, the star burned before us, pulling us onward.

At last we reached Jerusalem. Surely here, in the city of David, the King would be known. We asked with eager voices, "Where is the newborn King of the Jews? We have seen His star as it rose, and we have come to worship Him."

But instead of joy, unease rippled through the city. Whispers spread like fire. Soon we were summoned into Herod's palace.

The halls glittered with marble and gold. Incense hung thick in the air, and soldiers stood rigid in gleaming armor. Herod sat on his throne, his jeweled crown catching torchlight. His smile was thin, his eyes sharp.

When we spoke of a child born King, his face shadowed though his voice remained smooth. He summoned priests and scribes, who searched the sacred scrolls and declared, "In Bethlehem of Judea—for this is what the prophet wrote."

Herod leaned forward, his voice dropping to a feigned whisper of reverence: "Go to Bethlehem. Search carefully for the child. And when you find Him, come back and tell me, so that I too may go and worship Him."

We bowed, as custom required, but unease pressed upon us like a heavy cloak. Worship was not in his spirit. His throne was his only concern.

That night, we left Jerusalem. And there again was the star! Shining, brilliant, guiding us away from Herod's shadow and down into the quiet of Bethlehem.

The streets were simple, the homes plain, the night hushed. Then the star stopped—fixed above a small house. Our hearts pounded. After years of watching, months of journeying, we had come to the place.

We entered.

And there He was.

The Child. God's Son. Jesus!

His mother Mary cradled Him, His father Josheph nearby. No throne, no court, no jeweled crown. Yet the air felt alive, holy, as though heaven itself bent close. My knees gave way. Tears blurred my eyes. All the waiting, all the searching, all the miles—they led to this moment.

The First Magi – Gold

I stepped forward first, carrying a chest. Inside was gold, shining in the firelight. Gold was a gift for kings. It adorned crowns, built temples, filled treasuries. It was wealth, honor, and authority. To give gold was to proclaim a sovereign.

I knelt low, my heart trembling. "You are the true King," my soul whispered. "Greater than Caesar, greater than every ruler who has ever lived. Your throne will never fade. This gold is Yours—for You alone are worthy to reign."

The Second Magi – Frankincense

I followed, carrying a carved jar. As I opened it, the fragrance of frankincense filled the room, sharp and sweet, curling upward like prayer. Frankincense was rare, drawn from the tears of distant trees, used by priests in worship. Its smoke rose from temple altars as a symbol of prayers reaching God.

As the scent filled the small home, tears fell from my eyes. My soul whispered: "You are God with us. You are Emmanuel. This incense belongs not to idols, not to temples made with hands, but to You, the living God who has come to dwell among us. May my worship, my life, rise to You as this fragrance rises now."

The Third Magi – Myrrh

I was last, holding a vessel of myrrh. Its aroma was rich and bittersweet, heavy with meaning. Myrrh was drawn from resin like frankincense, but its use was solemn. It was used to soothe wounds, to heal pain, to perfume garments, and most of all, to anoint the dead. It spoke of both suffering and hope.

As I placed it before Him, my spirit surged as if it could no longer be contained. "You will bring healing to the nations," my heart cried. "Though suffering lies ahead, through You will come redemption. This gift is my trust that even in sorrow, life will flow. You are the Savior, the hope of all."

We bowed together, our faces to the ground, our treasures laid before Him. But more than treasures, our hearts were poured out in worship. Gold for His kingship. Frankincense for His divinity. Myrrh for His sacrifice. Each gift spoke what words could not.

The star had led us across the earth, but the true Light now shone from His face. We had found Him—the King of kings, the Son of God.

Scriptures: Matthew 2:1-12

Egypt

I REMEMBER THE NIGHT as though it were carved into my very soul. We had just laid our son down, His soft breathing filling the quiet, when the angel of the Lord came to me again in a dream. His voice was urgent, steady, and the world seemed to narrow around the force of his words: "Get up! Flee to Egypt with the child and His mother. Stay there until I tell you to return, because Herod is going to search for the child to kill Him."

I woke in a cold sweat, the weight of those words pressing on me. Kill Him? My Son—the Son of God? From the very beginning, the enemy has sought to destroy Him. I remembered the stories of Pharaoh ordering Hebrew babies drowned in the Nile, the serpent in Eden scheming against God's promise, and now Herod—a puppet of that same enemy—setting his eyes on my boy. My heart trembled, but faith held me steady. God had spoken, and I would obey.

In the dark of night, I roused Mary. Her eyes widened, fear flickering across her face as I told her what God had revealed. Without hesitation, she clutched Jesus close. There was no time to waste. I gathered what little we had, loaded the donkey, and we slipped into the night. Every shadow seemed to move, every sound pierced my ears. Danger was close, but the Lord was closer.

Mary later told me how her heart beat as she held Him tightly, every step of the journey a prayer whispered under her breath. She thought of the angel's words to her, of the promise that this child would be called the Son of the Most High. If God had spoken it, then God would surely preserve Him. Still, the tears came—tears for Bethlehem's children, tears for the mothers who would wail as their little ones were taken from them. Evil had always hunted the promise of God, but even through her grief, Mary held onto the truth: no plan of the enemy could undo the Word spoken over her Son.

The road to Egypt was long and harsh. I thought often of what lay behind us—innocent children in Bethlehem, families whose cries would soon pierce the heavens. My heart broke for them, even as I pressed forward with the weight of protecting the One who had come to save us all.

Egypt felt strange to me—its language, its customs, its idols. Yet even there, the Lord provided. I found work with my hands, laboring as I always had, shaping wood, mending tools, building shelter. Each day I saw how God sustained us. There was food on our table, a roof over our heads, and safety for my family. What the enemy meant for destruction, the Lord turned into provision.

And as I worked, I watched my son grow. Each morning, His laughter filled our home, and every evening He lay sleeping peacefully in Mary's arms. There were moments when I would pause in awe, the weight of it all pressing into me: this child, running barefoot across our floor, was the very Son of God. He captured my heart with every smile, every question in His eyes, every small hand that reached for mine.

Mary often whispered to me in the quiet of night, reflecting on the words spoken over Him. She remembered Gabriel's greeting, the shepherds' song, Simeon's prophecy, Anna's praise. "Joseph," she would say softly, "He is the promise—here, in our arms, in our home." There was joy in her voice, but also wonder, as if she too trembled at the mystery unfolding before us.

There was deep joy in watching Him grow, yet also a holy weight. We wondered what it would mean, how He would fulfill what was spoken, and what role we were to play. We did not have every answer, but we carried every word in our hearts, trusting the God who had spoken them. Even in exile, even in a foreign land, joy and faith filled our days. We were living within the story God had written long before us, and we could see it unfolding in the life of the child entrusted to our care—the One who would bring salvation to all.

Years later, the angel came again. "Herod is dead. It is safe." Relief swept over us, though we knew the world was still not safe for our Son. As we set out, another dream came—warning me not to settle in Judea, for Herod's son now ruled there with the same violence in his heart. So once more, we turned our steps, this time toward Galilee, returning to the small town of Nazareth where the Angel first spoke to Mary, although an unlikely place for the

Messiah to grow up—so ordinary, so hidden. Yet even this fulfilled what had been spoken by the prophets.

Again and again, we saw it: every twist, every detour, every unknown was not outside of God's plan. He was guiding our every step. The same God who had spoken through angels, through Scripture, through dreams, was weaving His purposes through our obedience. We had only to trust and walk forward.

We often reflected on how much of our lives had become a journey of faith into the unknown. From the moment Gabriel appeared, nothing was certain except this—God had spoken, and we would believe Him. Each day held questions we could not answer, dangers we could not foresee, and challenges we could not avoid. Yet through it all, there was a peace—His peace—that settled over us like a covering. It was not the peace of knowing every detail, but the peace of knowing the One who went before us.

As we built our life in Nazareth, raising Jesus in the quiet rhythms of work and family, we stood on the promises spoken to us. We remembered the shepherds' song of glory, Simeon's blessing, Anna's prophecy, the angel's words, and the Scriptures of old. We held them close, and they became the ground beneath our feet. And as we walked each day into the unknown, we discovered the shalom of God—the deep, unshakable peace that surpasses all understanding—because we knew He was with us and would never fail us.

Even in the ordinary days of Nazareth, we were living inside the extraordinary story of God. And in our hearts, we knew—what He had begun, He would bring to completion.

Scriptures: Matthew 2:13-23

The Relative

I WILL NEVER FORGET that Passover pilgrimage. Each year the journey itself was a kind of worship—families and neighbors traveling together, voices singing the Psalms of Ascent as we climbed toward Jerusalem. The air was filled with dust, laughter, and the steady rhythm of sandals striking stone. When we finally reached the city, it swelled with tens of thousands of pilgrims, lambs bleating, merchants shouting, the aroma of bread, spices, and sacrifices mingling in the streets. And at the heart of it all rose the Temple, white and gleaming, the place where the presence of God rested.

The courts of the Temple were for sacrifices, worship and teaching. There, under shaded colonnades, sat the teachers of the Law. These men were distinct from the Pharisees and Sadducees, though often confused with them. The Pharisees were strict in keeping traditions, interpreting the Law with great detail, sometimes adding rules upon rules as a fence around God's Word. The Sadducees, mostly wealthy priests, rejected many of the traditions the Pharisees clung to and did not believe in the resurrection of the dead. But the teachers of the Law—scribes and scholars—were the ones who studied, copied, and explained the Scriptures. Their task was to preserve God's Word, to interpret it carefully, and to pass it on. Some aligned themselves with Pharisees, others with Sadducees, but all were regarded as men of learning, custodians of the sacred texts.

What set the teachers of the Law apart, though, was not just their words but their appearance. They wore long flowing robes, often white or cream linen, with tassels at the corners as the Law commanded, reminders of God's covenant with Israel. Some were draped with prayer shawls that shimmered faintly in the sunlight. On their foreheads and arms they bound phylacteries—small leather boxes containing passages of the Torah—obeying the command to keep God's Word ever before their eyes and hands. Their beards were long and carefully kept, a sign of dignity and age, and their hair was worn in ways that marked them as men set apart, often with the side locks of devotion framing their faces. To us, they looked like walking reminders of the covenant God had made with our people. Their very presence commanded respect. Students sat at their feet with reverence, repeating their words in whispers, determined to remember every phrase. To carry the dust of a rabbi's sandals on your cloak was considered an honor—it meant you had walked closely with wisdom itself.

And it was among these teachers of the Law that we found Jesus. After three days of frantic searching—Mary with tear-stained cheeks, Joseph with shoulders bent under the weight of fear—we entered the courts and saw Him. There He sat, not lost at all, but right at home among the learned, His posture calm, His eyes alive.

He was listening, asking questions, giving answers that startled even the most seasoned. I saw the rabbis stroke their beards, pausing to think, nodding slowly at His words. Students stared wide-eyed at this boy who spoke with clarity that carried authority far beyond His age.

Mary's cry broke the moment, her voice trembling with a mixture of relief, anger, and overwhelming love: "Son, why have You done this to us? Your father and I have been frantic, searching for You everywhere!" I could hear in her tone both the fear of nearly losing Him and the exasperation of a mother whose heart could not bear another moment of uncertainty.

Joseph stood behind her, quiet, but his eyes were fixed on Jesus. I could almost see the thoughts stirring within him—wonder and amazement that his twelve-year-old son was not only sitting among the teachers of the Law but astonishing them with His wisdom. Joseph must have recalled the angel's words from years before, that this child was Immanuel, God with us. And now, before his very eyes, he was watching it unfold.

And then Jesus answered, His voice steady, innocent yet piercing: "But why did you need to search? Didn't you know that I must be in my Father's house?"

Those words seemed to still the air itself. Mary's tears slowed, but her brow furrowed with confusion. She remembered Gabriel's promise—that this child would be called the Son of the Most High. And yet, how could she reconcile her role as mother, her fear and worry, with this divine claim? She could not fully understand, but she treasured His words, holding them like a secret folded deep in her heart.

Joseph's face softened. He had come to the Temple filled with dread, but now he left pondering with awe. The boy he raised with his hands was revealing Himself as the One who came from the hands of God.

As we turned back toward Nazareth, Jesus walked beside them, obedient and untroubled. Yet Mary and Joseph's steps were slower, each of them carrying not only relief but the weight of mystery. They had found Him, yes—but they had also been reminded once more that He belonged first to God.

Scriptures: Luke 2:41-52

Ministry

30-33 AD

Andrew

THE DAYS OF TIBERIUS Caesar weighed heavy on us all. Fifteen years he had reigned, though Rome felt far away, its power pressed on every home. Pilate governed Judea with cruelty, Herod Antipas ruled Galilee, Philip reigned to the north, and Lysanias in Abilene. Even in Jerusalem, the high priesthood was stained—Annas and Caiaphas trading power like merchants bartering in the temple courts. Corruption, greed, and fear marked the times.

And yet, into this darkness, the word of God came—not to Caesar in his palace, not to Pilate in his fortress, not to Annas or Caiaphas in their robes—but to John, son of Zechariah, in the wilderness.

I had left the nets of Galilee for a time, restless for God, hungry for something real. That is where I found him. John stood like Elijah of old, clothed in camel's hair bound with a leather belt. His food was locusts and wild honey—simple, lawful, untouched by the corruption of the city. His very life was a protest against the pride of Jerusalem and the luxury of Rome. He belonged wholly to God.

And there was something different about him. His eyes carried a fire I had never seen in another man. His words were not polished like the teachers of the Law, yet every syllable struck the soul like thunder. His focus was unshakable, his zeal for God burned without pause. He was not distracted by comfort, not seduced by recognition. He lived only to please the One who had sent him. It was as if his very breath was consumed with the urgency of God's call.

His voice carried over the Jordan: "Repent of your sins and turn to God, for the Kingdom of Heaven is near!" Crowds poured into the desert from every direction—farmers, mothers with children, merchants, shepherds, soldiers, tax collectors, priests. Some came scoffing, others weeping, all of us drawn by the fire burning in this man.

Then John lifted his voice with the words of Isaiah, words that seemed to leap alive from centuries past:

"I am a voice shouting in the wilderness,
'Prepare the way for the Lord's coming!
Clear the road for him!
The valleys will be filled,
and the mountains and hills made level.
The curves will be straightened,
and the rough places made smooth.
And then all people will see
the salvation sent from God.'" (Luke 3:4-6 NLT)

In that moment, the wilderness trembled with more than sound. I saw hardened men break, weeping as they confessed their sins. Some cried out for forgiveness of greed that had ruled their dealings. Others fell to their knees, confessing idols they had trusted more than God. There were shouts of sorrow for stealing, for betraying friends, for turning blind eyes to the poor, for living only for self. Soldiers struck their chests, broken by the weight of their extortion and violence. Women sobbed for coldness in their hearts. Even children clung to their parents, as if they too felt the holiness of God pressing near.

The air filled with desperate cries: "Forgive me, Lord! Have mercy on me!" Many stumbled to the water's edge, tears cutting paths through the dust on their faces. Again and again John plunged them beneath the Jordan as they confessed aloud, rising from the waters with hearts made new. It was as though one great cry rose from the multitude: We are not ready. Make us ready. We need You, O Lord.

But not all hearts bowed. That was the day the Pharisees and Sadducees came, their robes spotless, their steps deliberate, their faces proud. They stood at the edge of the crowd as if judgment belonged to them. But John saw through their show. His voice flamed like a prophet's fire: "You brood of snakes! Who warned you to flee the coming wrath? Prove by the way you live that you have repented of your sins and turned to God. Don't just say to each other, 'We are safe, for we are descendants of Abraham.' For I tell you, God can create children of Abraham from these very stones.

Even now the axe of God's judgment is poised, ready to sever the roots of the trees. Yes, every tree that does not produce good fruit will be chopped down and thrown into the fire."

I saw their faces stiffen, jaws set, eyes flashing. They were used to honor, but in the wilderness John stripped them bare. His call was for all of us—Pharisee, soldier, beggar, priest, fisherman alike. No one would stand before God on titles or ancestry; only true repentance could prepare the way.

Still, John never pointed to himself. Again and again he reminded us: "I baptize you with water, but someone is coming soon who is greater than I am—so much greater that I'm not even worthy to be his slave and carry his sandals. He will baptize you with the Holy Spirit and with fire."

That day I understood more than ever: John's life was not his own. His clothing, his food, his voice, his whole being—it all burned with a single purpose: to prepare the way for the Messiah. To break the hardness of our hearts so we would not miss the One coming after him.

And as I stood among the multitude, watching men and women cry out to God with tears streaming down their faces, I felt the weight of it all. This was no ordinary movement, no passing revival of emotion. This was God Himself stirring His people, plowing up the hard ground of our hearts, making ready for something greater than we had ever known.

The wilderness seemed charged with holy fear. Every confession, every tear, every plunge beneath the waters of the Jordan carried a soberness I could not shake. It was as if heaven itself was bending low, urging us to see that these were not empty words, but the beginning of God's plan unfolding before our eyes.

For centuries we had prayed for the Messiah. Prophets had spoken, generations had waited, and many had died with only the hope of His coming. But now—now—the time was near. God had set His plan in motion, and nothing would stop it. John was the forerunner, the herald, the voice crying out. And his cry demanded everything of us: no more living for self, no more chasing idols, no more empty rituals. This was the moment to repent, to surrender, to yield fully to the Lord.

Shock and urgency ran through me as the truth settled in. We were not simply preparing for another prophet, another teacher, or another leader. We were preparing for the very Son of God—the Lamb who would take away the sins of the world. And if our hearts were not made ready, we would miss Him.

The air that day felt heavy with eternity. Every word John spoke, every cry that rose from the people, every splash of water in the Jordan—it all carried the weight of heaven's purpose. God's plan, written from the foundation of the world, was breaking into time. The Messiah was about to step onto the stage of history, and nothing would ever be the same again.

In that soberness, I trembled. My soul longed, my spirit burned, and I knew—I had to be ready. We all had to be ready.

For the Lamb of God was near.

And then, on a day like no other, He came. Jesus of Nazareth walked down to the Jordan. I can still see Him stepping through the crowd, not with the pride of a ruler nor the pomp of a priest, but with a quiet authority that seemed to draw every eye. The people hushed, the air shifted, and John himself grew still as he saw Him approaching. Then with a voice both trembling and sure, John lifted his hand and declared, "Look! The Lamb of God who takes away the sin of the world!"

The crowd parted as Jesus stepped into the water. John faltered, whispering, "I am the one who needs to be baptized by You. So why are You coming to me?"

But Jesus said, "It should be done, for we must carry out all that God requires."

John lowered Him into the Jordan, and as Jesus rose, heaven itself tore open. Light poured down brighter than the desert sun. The Spirit descended like a dove, resting upon Him. And then the voice came, shaking the earth and the soul alike: "You are my dearly loved Son, and you bring me great joy."

I fell to my knees, overwhelmed. Around me people cried out, some wept openly, others stood frozen in awe. God had spoken. Heaven had opened. The Messiah had been revealed.

I knew my life would never be the same.

Scriptures: Matthew 3:1-16, Mark 1:1-11, Luke 3:1-22 and John 1:29-34

The Angel

FOR FORTY DAYS I watched Him. The Beloved Son, clothed in frail humanity, yet filled with the Spirit without measure. The wilderness was harsh—rock and dust, silence broken only by the cries of wild beasts. The sun scorched by day, the cold pierced by night. Hunger gnawed at His body, yet His gaze never wavered from the Father.

All through those forty days and nights, the enemy came. Whisper after whisper, dart after dart, Satan tempted Him relentlessly—trying to exploit His hunger, His weariness, His solitude. The deceiver hoped to find a crack, a weakness, some small way to draw Him into sin and break the purpose for which He came. Yet again and again, the Son resisted, clinging to the Word of God.

When the long fast drew to its end, Satan made his boldest assault. I watched as he came with his first great snare. His voice was smooth, filled with lies dressed as reason: "If you are the Son of God, tell these stones to become loaves of bread." The ground was littered with rocks—jagged, dry, lifeless. My being ached at the thought of His hunger. With a single word, He could have feasted. Yet He lifted His head, eyes burning with resolve, and spoke, "No!

The Scriptures say, 'People do not live by bread alone, but by every word that comes from the mouth of God.'" His voice carried the thunder of truth, and Satan's smile faltered.

Unyielding, the deceiver swept Him to the heights of the Temple in Jerusalem. The city below bustled unaware. I saw the enemy twist the very words of Scripture, daring Him to leap: "If you are the Son of God, jump off! For the Scriptures say, 'He will order his angels to protect you. And they will hold you up with their hands so you won't even hurt your foot on a stone.'" How it sickened me, hearing our sacred charge used as bait! We stood ready, for yes, the Father had promised His care. But Jesus, steady and unwavering, answered, "The Scriptures also say, 'You must not test the Lord your God.'" His words struck like fire, and again the tempter recoiled.

Yet Satan would not relent. From the wilderness to a mountain's height, he unveiled a vision of kingdoms—nations glittering with wealth and power, thrones and armies at his command. The world lay before his like a prize. The adversary whispered, "I will give it all to you if you will kneel down and worship me." My spirit burned with holy rage at such arrogance—to demand the Creator bow to the created! The air itself grew tense as heaven waited for His reply. With holy fire in His voice, He declared, "Get out of here, Satan! For the Scriptures say, 'You must worship the Lord your God and serve only Him.'"

At that command, the enemy shrieked, powerless to remain. The air that moments before had carried the stench of deception was suddenly clean and still. Darkness scattered, and the mountain was quiet again. All of creation seemed to breathe in relief, as though the very stones understood that the Son of God had stood firm. The serpent had tried with all his cunning to break Him at His weakest moment, but every scheme had failed.

It was then we were released. With swiftness and reverence, we drew near Him. We carried bread, cool water, and the strength of heaven itself. But more than food, we brought the Father's comfort. As we touched His weary frame—trembling hands and a body hollowed by fasting—we strengthened Him. Yet in truth, our hearts trembled more than His flesh. For in His eyes burned a holy fire, fierce and tender all at once. He had chosen the Father's will over His own hunger, His own safety, and the fleeting glory of the world. In that choosing, He had already secured the pathway of salvation for all who would believe.

And just as He had entered this wilderness full of the Holy Spirit, He now stood at the end of forty days of testing—strong, resolute, and radiant with the Spirit's power. Satan's temptations had not weakened Him; they had only revealed the depth of His obedience and the purity of His love for the Father.

As we ministered, awe overwhelmed us. We had sung at the dawn of creation, but never had we seen such beauty in obedience. We had watched kingdoms rise and fall, but never had we seen such authority wielded with such humility. We had beheld the throne of heaven, but now we saw heaven's King clothed in frailty, victorious not by force but by surrender to the Father's will. Our hearts burned with worship, and though our hands served Him, it was we who were overcome in His presence..

This was not merely the triumph of a moment—it was a victory that would echo into eternity. For here in the wilderness, the Son had stood where Adam had fallen, and the way of salvation was assured. We knew then that the cross would come, the tomb would open, and the serpent's head would be crushed forever. And we, the servants of the Most High, counted it the deepest honor of heaven to have witnessed such glory.

Scriptures: Matthew 4:1-11, Luke 4:1-13

The First Day

Andrew's First Day with Jesus

THE JORDAN'S WATERS STILL lingered in my memory—John's voice ringing out, "Look! There is the Lamb of God!" That moment had pierced me, for when I turned and saw Jesus, everything within me knew He was the One. His eyes looked straight through me yet covered me with love. His voice—gentle, inviting—spoke, "What do you want?" And when I stumbled out my simple reply, His answer burned into my soul: "Come and see."

We stayed with Him that day. The hours slipped away like minutes, His words carrying life itself. The warmth of the fire, the peace in the room, the sound of His voice—it was as if heaven had touched earth. My heart knew: I had found the Messiah. I ran to Simon and told him, "We have found the Messiah!" And when I brought him to Jesus, the Lord looked at him and said, "You are Simon, son of John. You will be called Cephas." Even in that moment, Jesus spoke destiny into my brother's life.

After a few days, Simon and I returned to the work we had always known on the Sea of Galilee. The smell of fish clung to our clothes, and our hands were raw from hauling nets that seemed heavier with each cast. All through the night we labored—backs aching, nets empty, hearts weary.

Then Jesus came. The morning light shimmered on the lake as the crowd pressed close to hear Him. His words carried power, drawing men like the tide draws the sea. He stepped into Simon's boat and asked us to push out a little from shore. We obeyed, and as He sat teaching, the sound of His voice rose above the lapping water. Every word He spoke stirred something in me deeper than the nets we held.

When He finished speaking, He turned to Simon with a intentional gaze: "Now go out where it is deeper, and let down your nets to catch some fish."

I felt Simon tense beside me. His voice carried the frustration of the long night: "Master, we worked hard all last night and didn't catch a thing. But if you say so, I'll let the nets down again."

The rope slipped through our hands, the nets sank into the water, and suddenly—life exploded beneath the surface. The weight nearly pulled us under. My arms burned as we struggled to pull in the catch. The nets strained and tore, fish flailed and leapt, the boats creaked under the load. We shouted for help, and James and John rushed to us, their boat filling too. Never had I seen such abundance!

Simon fell to his knees before Jesus, his voice trembling, "Oh, Lord, please leave me—I'm such a sinful man." My own heart echoed the same. Standing before such holiness, I felt the depth of my unworthiness.

But Jesus—His voice was not condemning, not harsh. His eyes were full of love. He spoke words that lifted us from despair to destiny: "Don't be afraid! From now on you'll be fishing for people!"

The power of His words broke me open. They weren't just sounds on the air; they were life reshaping my very soul. In that moment, everything else faded—the boats, the fish, the business, the life we had always known. We left it all on the shore, nets tangled and fish flopping in the boats, and followed Him.

Simon, James, John, and I—we walked away from everything, not out of duty, but because His heart drew us with a love stronger than the sea. His voice still echoes in me: "Come and see. Follow me. Don't be afraid."

I, Andrew, once only a fisherman, had seen the Messiah. His words had called me out of the ordinary into the eternal. My life would never be the same.

Scriptures: John 1:35-50, Matthew 4:18-22, Mark 1:19-20 and Luke 5:1-11

Hometown

I GREW UP IN Nazareth. To most of the world, our little village hardly mattered. People would scoff and say, "Can anything good come out of Nazareth?" But it was home to me. Life here was plain and rugged, shaped by the rocky hills and the dry Galilean wind.

Our days were full of labor. The men rose early to tend the fields, vineyards, and olive groves. Shepherds led flocks out at dawn, their voices carrying through the hills as they called to their sheep. Women carried water jars from the well, their laughter mingling with the clatter of clay pots and the smell of baking bread. Children ran the narrow, dusty paths, kicking up stones with their bare feet. Life was hard under Rome's rule—we felt the weight of their taxes and the sting of their soldiers' presence when they passed nearby—but in Nazareth, we leaned on each other, living as tightly woven families.

It was in this small village that Jesus grew up. His family was like ours: simple, hardworking, devoted to God. Joseph, His father, was a carpenter. I remember the sound of his mallet striking wood, echoing from their little workshop, the shavings that littered the floor, the smell of fresh-cut cedar and olive wood. Joseph built tables and doors, yokes for oxen, beams for roofs—strong, dependable work.

And Jesus was always there. I can still see Him as a boy, carrying wood on His shoulder, sweat on His brow, but never complaining. There was something steady in Him, something different. He played with us children, but He never seemed to get swept up in foolishness or cruelty. His words were kind. His eyes carried a depth that made you feel known, even as a child. Still, to us, He was just Jesus, Joseph's son—the carpenter's boy with brothers and sisters like any other family in the village.

Years passed. Jesus grew into manhood, worked in His father's shop, and then—He left. We didn't hear much until rumors began to spread. Strange rumors. They said He was teaching in the synagogues of Galilee with authority that shocked the rabbis. They said He was healing the sick, casting out unclean spirits, even opening blind eyes. Crowds followed Him wherever He went. Some whispered He was the Messiah. Others said He was a prophet. Many simply didn't know what to make of Him.

When word reached Nazareth that Jesus was coming home, the whole village stirred. Curiosity filled us. We had known Him since He was a boy. We had seen Him at work in Joseph's shop. Could it really be true? Could the carpenter's son be the one chosen by God?

On the Sabbath, the synagogue was crowded. The men sat shoulder to shoulder, women and children nearby. The familiar smell of parchment and oil lamps filled the room. We murmured in anticipation as Jesus stood. The attendant handed Him the scroll of Isaiah, and He began to read.

His voice was steady, yet it carried weight that silenced the room:

"The Spirit of the Lord is upon me,
for he has anointed me to bring Good News to the poor.
He has sent me to proclaim that captives will be released,
that the blind will see,
that the oppressed will be set free,
and that the time of the Lord's favor has come."
(Luke 4:18–19 NLT)

When He finished, He rolled up the scroll, gave it back to the attendant, and sat down. Every eye in the synagogue was fixed on Him. Then He spoke again: "The Scripture you've just heard has been fulfilled this very day."

The words struck me like lightning. Fulfilled? Here? Now? By Him? For a moment, we were amazed—awed at the grace in His words, the authority He carried. But quickly, the murmurs rose.

"Isn't this Joseph's son?" someone scoffed.
"We know His brothers—James, Joseph, Simon, Judas. His sisters live here among us," another said.
"Where did He get such wisdom? Such power?"

I wrestled inside myself. I remembered Him as a boy, my neighbor, as a young man at the carpenter's bench. Could this same Jesus truly be the Messiah?

Then He spoke again, and His words pierced us. He reminded us of Elijah, sent not to Israel, but to a widow in Zarephath, a Gentile. He spoke of Elisha healing Naaman the Syrian, not an Israelite. It was as if He was saying God's mercy extended beyond us—to outsiders, to those we thought unworthy. His words unsettled me, challenged me. But for many, they ignited rage.

The synagogue erupted. Men leapt to their feet, shouting, their faces twisted with fury. "How dare He speak this way!" some cried. "Does He insult His own people? Does He think He's greater than the prophets?"

I was swept up in the mob as they seized Him, dragging Him out of the synagogue and toward the steep cliff at the edge of town. My stomach churned. My mind raced. Part of me wanted to silence Him, to push Him away, to protect the walls of what I thought I understood. But another part of me trembled, wondering if what He spoke was truth, if God Himself was walking among us.

We reached the cliff. The air was thick with fury, the shouts of my neighbors ringing in my ears. But then, in a way I cannot explain, Jesus turned. He looked at us—not with fear, not with anger, but with eyes full of strength and sorrow. And somehow, He passed through the crowd. Our hands could not hold Him. Our rage could not touch Him. He walked away, calm and steady, leaving us stunned.

I stood there, breathless, my heart pounding. That day has never left me. I had known Jesus my whole life. I had eaten bread with Him, watched Him work with His father, seen Him walk our dusty roads. And yet, when He revealed Himself, I could not accept it. None of us could.

Even now, I wrestle. Could it be that in our familiarity, we missed the very One we prayed for? That in our pride, we could not see God's answer standing in front of us?

I still see His eyes in my memory—eyes that knew me, eyes that ached for us. And I wonder if the boy we thought we knew was the Savior we had always longed for.

Scriptures: Luke 4:14-28, Matthew 13:54-58 and Mark 6:1-6

The Wedding Servant

THE MORNING OF THE wedding was unlike any other day. A wedding in our village was not just about a man and woman being joined together—it was a holy covenant, a symbol of God's own love for His people. In our Jewish tradition, marriage was more than a celebration; it echoed the promises of the Lord. Just as Israel was called God's bride, so a wedding reminded us that covenant is sacred, binding, and filled with hope for generations to come.

The bridegroom had spent months preparing—building a place for his bride, making sure everything was ready to welcome her into his home. His return to bring her was a picture of joy and faithfulness, and we all knew these weddings could last a full week, with day after day of feasting, laughter, and dancing. To host generously was a matter of honor; to fail in this brought shame that could cling to a family for years. Wine, especially, was more than drink—it was the very symbol of joy, blessing, and abundance. To run out of wine was to run out of joy itself, a humiliation no bridegroom ever wanted to face.

As a servant, I had risen before dawn to prepare for this day. The courtyard was alive with motion: the smell of lamb roasting, bread baking, figs and olives laid out in baskets. Jars of water stood ready for ceremonial washing, for purity was never taken lightly. Guests soon arrived in their finest garments—women with veils draped gracefully, men laughing as they greeted one another, children darting about with shouts of excitement. Musicians tuned their flutes and tambourines, and garlands of flowers hung above the entrance to welcome all who came.

I knew my place well. It was my duty to serve, to fill cups before they were empty, to keep bread on the tables, to ensure every guest felt honored. Hospitality was not optional—it was a sacred duty. Every detail mattered. A feast was not only for the bride and groom but for the honor of their families, and ultimately, for the glory of God who blessed covenant love.

Yet beneath the joy of that day lay an unspoken tension. Whispers began to spread among us servants—the wine was running out. At first, I hoped it was only a rumor, but the urgency in the steward's face confirmed it. I felt a surge of alarm. For all the music and laughter, disgrace was near. Running out of wine was not a small thing—it was shame, a mark of failure. And I, standing there with empty jars, felt powerless to stop it.

That was when I noticed Mary, the mother of Jesus. She had been moving quietly among the guests, but now I saw her speak with Him. Her eyes were full of calm confidence, though her words carried urgency. She said, "They have no more wine."

Jesus looked at her with a tenderness I cannot forget, but His reply puzzled me: "Dear woman, that's not our problem. My time has not yet come."

I glanced at her, expecting disappointment. But she didn't falter. She turned toward us servants, her voice steady and certain, and said, "Do whatever He tells you."

Her words struck me. There was no doubt in her tone, no hesitation. She believed He would act, even though His words seemed to say otherwise. In that moment, I felt caught between confusion and expectancy, my heart pounding with questions I dared not speak.

Then Jesus looked at us servants. His voice was calm, yet it carried a sacred weight that seemed to bow my soul in reverence. He said, 'Fill the jars with water."

I turned and saw the six stone jars standing nearby. They were massive vessels, each holding twenty to thirty gallons, carved thick and heavy so they would not easily crack. Even empty, they took strength to shift. These jars were not for drinking or for wine—they were for ceremonial washing. According to our customs, guests would dip water from them to cleanse their hands before eating, a reminder of God's holiness and the purity He desired for His people. To us, these vessels were symbols of the old ways, of the law and the cleansing traditions passed down from our fathers.

And now, Jesus told us to fill them? My mind wrestled with the command. Water jars meant for purification, now to be used for wine? It felt strange, almost improper. But Mary's words rang in my ears: Do whatever He tells you. So we obeyed.

We hurried, carrying bucket after bucket, until each jar was filled to the very brim. My arms ached, sweat ran down my back, but with each pour, an expectancy grew within me, though I could not explain why.

Then He spoke again. "Now dip some out, and take it to the master of ceremonies."

I froze. Take water to the master? Surely he would be furious. Yet as I dipped the ladle, I noticed it—the liquid shimmered, darker than before. Could it be? I carried the cup with trembling hands and offered it.

The master lifted the cup to his lips, and I held my breath as though the whole world hung on that single sip. My palms were damp, my stomach knotted, and I half expected him to spit it out in anger. But instead, his eyes widened, and joy spread across his face. He called for the bridegroom and said, "A host always serves the best wine first. Then, when everyone has had a lot to drink, he brings out the less expensive wine. But you have kept the best until now!"

The guests laughed with joy, raising their cups high, the celebration bursting with new life. Music and dancing filled the air once again, but I stood frozen, my heart pounding so loudly I could barely hear them.

I knew what had gone into those jars. Water. Ordinary water. I had drawn it, bucket by bucket, until my arms ached and sweat soaked my tunic. Yet here was the master of ceremonies praising it as the finest wine he had ever tasted. It made no sense. And yet, the evidence was undeniable.

My thoughts spun wildly. Who was this man—Jesus? With just His word, He had turned water into wine. Not just wine, but the best wine. Abundance overflowing from jars once reserved for ritual washing. Something inside me stirred, like the first crack of dawn breaking through the night.

As the laughter and dancing grew around me, I could hardly move. My fellow servants glanced at one another, eyes wide with awe. We had no words, but we shared the same knowing—we had seen something holy. The guests were oblivious, too busy celebrating, but we knew. We had watched water become wine before our very eyes.

A strange mixture of emotions flooded me—fear, wonder, joy, and something deeper I could not yet name. I felt small, as though I were standing on holy ground, unworthy even to have carried that cup. And yet I also felt seen, as if this miracle was not just for the wedding, not just for the guests, but for me. For us servants who had obeyed, who had filled the jars, who now carried this secret in our hearts.

It was as though Jesus was whispering through the miracle itself: "I take the ordinary, and I make it extraordinary. I take emptiness, and I fill it to overflowing. I take shame, and I turn it into honor."

My eyes stung with tears, though I quickly brushed them away. No one else seemed to notice what had happened, but I would never be the same. In silence, I watched Jesus with His disciples, their faces lit with the same awe I felt. There was something about Him—something beyond what I could explain—that drew me in, made me want to know more, to follow wherever He might lead.

That day, the wedding feast went on with laughter and joy, but for me, the true celebration was in my heart. I had witnessed glory—His glory—unveiled in the simplest of ways, yet it shook me to the core.

I came to the wedding as a servant, just doing my duty. I left knowing I had seen the hand of God at work through Jesus. And though life would carry on, I would never forget the day water was transformed into wine, became rich and full as wine, took on the deep crimson of wine—and my heart awoke to hope.

Scriptures: John 2:1-12 NLT

The Tax Collector

THE DAY BEGAN LIKE so many others for me. The sun was already climbing, its heat pressing against the back of my neck as I sat at my booth. Dust rose from the road as merchants led their donkeys past, their voices carrying sharp tones as they haggled over goods. I could hear the shuffling of sandals, the creak of wooden carts, and every now and then, I caught the low hiss of curses thrown in my direction. Some would not meet my eyes. Others spat on the ground as they passed.

My booth was cluttered with scrolls, wax tablets, and piles of coins—Roman denarii clinking against the shekels of my own people. That sound—sharp, metallic, heavy—was the music of my trade. I knew it well, and so did everyone else. For I was Matthew, a tax collector.

To the Romans, I was a useful man. To my own people, I was a traitor. Rome demanded its tribute: land taxes from farmers, customs from merchants, head taxes from every man. Once, our giving had been holy—tithes of grain, wine, oil, and livestock brought to the temple, offerings for the priests, the poor, and the house of God. Even the temple tax, though weighty, was part of worship.

But now, under Rome, taxes had become the yoke of oppression. Rome auctioned the right to collect them, and men like me were hired to gather the payments. The system was ripe for greed. Collect more than Rome required, and the excess lined our own pockets.

Most did. Most became wealthy, despised, and feared. Even if I told myself I wasn't as corrupt as the others, it made no difference. To my people, I was lumped in with thieves and harlots. The Pharisees considered me unclean, unworthy to enter the synagogue. My family's eyes grew cold when I walked into a room. And every coin I touched seemed to weigh down my soul with shame.

It was in the midst of this—another ordinary day of coins and curses—that He came.

Jesus.

I had heard His name murmured in the marketplace. Stories of healings, of miracles, of words that carried the breath of God Himself. I never imagined He would come near me. And yet, there He was, walking toward my booth.

The noise of the street seemed to hush. His eyes found mine—not with contempt, but with a piercing kindness that unsettled me. It was as though He saw straight through the walls I had built, straight into the ache I tried so hard to hide.

Then He spoke. Only two words, yet they changed everything: "Follow me."

A rush of wonder filled me. My hands hovered above the coins, trembling with anticipation. I glanced at the money, at the security I had clung to, at the life that had bought me wealth but cost me my soul. Then I looked back at Him. And something broke free inside me. Without another thought, I pushed back the stool, left the coins where they lay, and stepped out from behind the booth.

I followed Him.

That afternoon, I could not keep the joy contained. I wanted to honor Him, to show my gratitude, to open my life to Him the only way I knew how—by preparing a feast. As I walked home, my thoughts churned. What could I offer this man? My hands trembled as I told my servants to bring out the best—fresh bread, jars of wine, lamb seasoned with garlic and herbs. The scent filled the air as the fire crackled. I rearranged cushions, smoothed the table coverings, paced the floor. My heart raced with every step. He was coming. Jesus, the one who carried God's authority, was coming under my roof.

But then the doubt crept in—who would sit with us? My only friends were men like me: tax collectors, sinners, outcasts. Men hardened by rejection, their eyes tired from years of being shunned. They were all I had. A heaviness stirred inside me. Would He sit with us? Would He truly share a meal with people like us?

Still, I sent word. I invited them. Perhaps if they looked into His eyes as I had, perhaps if they heard His voice, they too might feel the hope rising in me.

As the evening came, the house filled with voices and laughter. The smell of roasted lamb mingled with the sweetness of wine. My friends arrived one by one, their laughter cautious at first, but soon filling the room. I felt joy swelling in me, though trembling too, for this was not just another dinner—it was my life laid bare before Him.

And then He entered. Jesus. The room fell silent for a breath, all eyes watching. My friends shifted uneasily, unsure how a teacher of Israel would treat us. But He smiled. He reclined at the table, at home among us, as though we truly belonged there with Him.

For a while, it was laughter and stories. The warmth of the lamps glowed, cups clinked, bread was broken, and peace wrapped itself around us like a cloak. But then, from outside, I heard them—the Pharisees. Their whispers carried sharp as knives: "Why does your teacher eat with such scum? With tax collectors and sinners?"

Their words pierced me, stirring a deep ache inside. They had called me that all my life. Scum. Unclean. A sinner beyond hope. And part of me wondered if they were right—should He even be here?

But before the weight crushed me, His voice cut through the murmur. Steady. Strong. Tender. "Healthy people don't need a doctor—sick people do."

The room stilled. My friends froze. The Pharisees' jaws clenched. Jesus' gaze moved toward them, and His next words carried both authority and compassion: "Now go and learn the meaning of this Scripture: 'I want you to show mercy, not offer sacrifices.' For I have come to call not those who think they are righteous, but those who know they are sinners."

The words hit me like a flood. I knew that Scripture—Hosea's cry: "I want you to show love, not offer sacrifices. I want you to know me more than I want burnt offerings." I had grown up hearing it, but I had long been shut out of the temple system, unwelcome in the synagogue, cut off from the offerings and rituals of worship. The Pharisees had barred me.

But Jesus was saying something entirely different. God's desire wasn't sacrifices I could never give—it was mercy. It was love. It was knowing Him.

Tears burned my eyes. For the first time, I felt the heart of God for me—not through rituals I couldn't touch, but through mercy sitting at my table.

I looked around the room at my friends. Their faces, so often hardened by shame, now softened with hope. Jesus had not only called me, He had called us.

That night, the words of Hosea lived again. Mercy had come to my house. Love was reclining at my table. And I knew—I would never be the same.

Scriptures: Matthew 9:9-13, Mark 2:13-17, Luke 5:27-32, Hosea 6:6

Tyre

LIFE IN TYRE WAS loud, busy, and unrelenting. The salty wind from the sea carried the cries of merchants bartering, the crack of whips on beasts of burden, and the clang of shipbuilders' hammers. Tyre was proud, rich in trade, filled with goods from Egypt, Greece, and beyond. But for families like ours, life was heavy.

I labored long hours on the docks, unloading goods that made other men rich. My hands were raw from ropes and timber, my back bent under weight that earned just enough for bread and dried fish. My wife kept a small stall in the marketplace, but louder sellers pushed her aside, and dishonest buyers often cheated her. Our children played in the alleys, but even their laughter couldn't quiet my fears of what kind of life we were giving them.

We often wondered if God even saw people like us. And then came the whispers. A man from Galilee. A healer. A prophet, perhaps even more. He touched the sick and they were well. He spoke words with authority that silenced the scholars. His name was Jesus.

At first, I brushed it off. Sailors always brought tales, and most of them faded as quickly as they came. But more stories reached our ears. And then my wife looked at me one evening across the flickering oil lamp. "We cannot stay here," she whispered. "If even part of this is true—if the Messiah has come—we must see Him for ourselves."

I wrestled with fear. If I left my work, we would lose wages. She would lose her place in the market. Even possibly lose my job. And we didn't even know where we were going—just setting out to search for this man, asking strangers along the way if they had heard of Jesus and where He might be. To take our children on such a journey without certainty seemed reckless. But her eyes shone with a faith I couldn't ignore.

So we went. Each morning we stopped travelers heading the opposite way. "Have you heard of a man called Jesus?" Some shook their heads, others said yes—He was in Capernaum, or near the lake, or in a nearby village. By the time we arrived, He had moved on. Our children grew weary, their feet blistered, yet their ears perked whenever someone spoke His name.

I remember meeting an old man by a well. His face was weathered like stone, but his eyes lit up when we spoke of Jesus. "I saw Him heal a man's withered hand," he said, voice trembling. "It was no trick—strength flowed back before my eyes." His words gave us courage to press on.

But there were long stretches of silence, too—days when no one knew, when doubt whispered in my ear. One night, as we rested beneath an olive tree, my son asked, "Abba, what if we never find Him?" My heart ached, for I had wondered the same. I pulled him close and said, "We will not stop searching. If He is who they say He is, He will be found."

Scriptures: Matthew chapters 5, 6 and 7 and Luke 6:17–49

The Mount

FINALLY, WE REACHED A hillside overlooking the Sea of Galilee. The sound reached us before the sight—the low murmur of thousands gathered, the laughter of children, the rise and fall of many voices blending together like the sea below. Wonder and determination filled us as we pressed forward, our children's hands clutched tightly, guiding them safely through the crowd. Farmers in rough tunics smelling of earth, fishermen with the tang of the sea still clinging to them, mothers cradling infants, elders leaning on staffs. I heard accents from Judea, Jerusalem, the Decapolis—and even some from our own Phoenicia. It felt as if the whole world had come.

For three days we had journeyed with our children, stopping often to ask where Jesus could be found. At last, we saw the great crowd gathered on the hillside, and my heart soared. We had traveled so far from Tyre, worn and dusty from the long journey, not even knowing where He might be. Yet, here He was, seated upon the slope, the breeze carrying His words over the multitude. People pressed in close, others sitting farther down the hill, yet every face was turned toward Him, waiting.

Then we saw Him and He saw us.

He was nothing like I had imagined. No robe of splendor, no crown upon His head, no guards to hold back the crowd. His garment was plain, His hands the rough hands of a laborer. Yet His face... His face carried both strength and tenderness, as though heaven itself rested in His gaze.

My wife's grip tightened around my hand, tears streaming unchecked. "It's Him," she whispered.

Our children stared in silence, wide-eyed. My youngest tugged at my sleeve and whispered, "Abba... He looks kind."

I swallowed hard, for it was true. One glance from Him, and I felt as though He saw everything—my weariness, my fears, my sins, my hunger. And instead of shame, I felt hope.

We found a place among the rocks and grass. The children leaned against us, their eyes never leaving Him. Slowly, the murmurs faded, until the hillside lay hushed, the only sound the wind whispering through the grass.

And then He opened His mouth and began to teach.

Jesus went up on the mountainside and sat down. His disciples gathered around him, and he began to teach them.

'God blesses those who are poor and realize their need for him, for the Kingdom of Heaven is theirs.

God blesses those who mourn, for they will be comforted.

God blesses those who are humble, for they will inherit the whole earth.

God blesses those who hunger and thirst for justice, for they will be satisfied.

God blesses those who are merciful, for they will be shown mercy.

God blesses those whose hearts are pure, for they will see God.

God blesses those who work for peace, for they will be called the children of God.

God blesses those who are persecuted for doing right, for the Kingdom of Heaven is theirs.

God blesses you when people mock you and persecute you and lie about you and say all sorts of evil things against you because you are my followers. Be happy about it! Be very glad! For a great reward awaits you in heaven. And remember, the ancient prophets were persecuted in the same way.'" (Matthew 5:1-12 NLT)

The words pierced me. It was as if He spoke directly into my soul. I looked at my wife, and tears welled in her eyes. She clutched the children close, whispering, "Did you hear? This is truth."

Around us were people from every corner of the land—farmers, fishermen, women with babies, elders, merchants with the dust of roads still on their sandals, and even those who looked wealthy, their robes clean and fine. Yet in that moment, we were all the same. All of us were hungry for something more.

I could feel the longing, the ache in every heart—poor and rich alike—as His voice rolled over us. His words carried a weight, but also a gentleness, like cool water poured into parched places of the soul.

I thought of my own weariness, the wages lost in leaving our work behind in Tyre, the risk of my employer never taking me back. But here, listening to Him, it didn't matter. Every word burned like fire inside of me, awakening a hope I had never known.

My wife whispered again, "He speaks as if Heaven is near."

And I believed her.

The people lingered in silence as His last words about reward in heaven echoed over the hillside. The air itself seemed alive—charged, yet peaceful. Then His voice rose again, steady and clear.

"You are the salt of the earth. But what good is salt if it has lost its flavor? Can you make it salty again? It will be thrown out and trampled underfoot as worthless.

You are the light of the world—like a city on a hilltop that cannot be hidden. No one lights a lamp and then puts it under a basket. Instead, a lamp is placed on a stand, where it gives light to everyone in the house. In the same way, let your good deeds shine out for all to see, so that everyone will praise your heavenly Father." (Matthew 5:13-16 NLT)

His words struck deep into me. Salt... light... I had always thought of myself as just a laborer from Tyre, my wife a mother tending children, our lives simple and small. Yet He spoke as if we mattered to the whole earth, as if the way we lived carried meaning beyond what our eyes could see.

I turned my gaze over the vast crowd—so many faces. A fisherman sat nearby, his hair still stiff with dried saltwater; a young boy clutched a crust of bread, nibbling as he listened; a man who looked like a scholar from Jerusalem stroked his beard thoughtfully; even a Roman soldier stood at the edge of the crowd, arms crossed, his stern face softened with curiosity. And yet, all of us—every one—He called to be salt and light.

I felt my wife's hand slip into mine. She whispered, "Can it be? That He is telling us—us—that we are part of God's plan for the world?"

I nodded, my throat tight. For years I had thought my days were spent only to earn bread, to pay debts, to work and to sleep. But now... now I sensed a calling, a weight that was both sobering and freeing.

I could almost see it—the city on a hill, shining in the night, unhidden, unmistakable. And I longed for our lives to be like that, for our children to walk in that light.

The sun glowed warm upon the hillside, and yet it was His words that truly lit my soul.

The hillside seemed to hold its breath as He paused. People shifted slightly, but no one dared rise or turn away. It was as if every word He spoke was water to our thirsty souls, and we feared missing even one drop. The sound of children playing in the distance hushed, and the murmurs of the crowd settled into stillness again.

After speaking of salt and light, His gaze moved over us, His voice firm yet filled with compassion. It was as though He could see into the hearts of the people—the poor, the weary, the seekers, even the skeptical. Then He spoke again, His words flowing like a stream, yet cutting deeper than any blade.

"Don't misunderstand why I have come. I did not come to abolish the law of Moses or the writings of the prophets. No, I came to accomplish their purpose. I tell you the truth, until heaven and earth disappear, not even the smallest detail of God's law will disappear until its purpose is achieved.

So if you ignore the least commandment and teach others to do the same, you will be called the least in the Kingdom of Heaven. But anyone who obeys God's laws and teaches them will be called great in the Kingdom of Heaven.

But I warn you—unless your righteousness is better than the righteousness of the teachers of religious law and the Pharisees, you will never enter the Kingdom of Heaven!" (Matthew 5:17-20 NLT)

A low murmur rippled through the crowd. The Pharisees and teachers of the Law—those men we had always been taught to revere as holy, untouchable in their devotion—He was saying that unless our righteousness surpassed theirs, we would not enter the Kingdom of Heaven?

My wife's eyes widened, and she whispered, "How could anyone be more righteous than they?"

The thought gripped me as well. All my life I had looked up to those men in their flowing robes, their long prayers, their stern warnings in the synagogues. Yet Jesus spoke as though righteousness was not a garment to be displayed, but a life transformed from within.

I thought of His earlier words—about being pure in heart, about hungering for justice, about showing mercy. Could it be that this was the righteousness He spoke of? Not the outward display, but an inward reality?

I squeezed my wife's hand, feeling the weight of His words press into me. Around us, some nodded in understanding, others looked troubled, and still others sat stunned, unable to speak. But for me, His words lit a fire inside, a holy ache to know more, to follow deeper.

I realized then that He wasn't just teaching us rules. He was unveiling the very heart of God.

The crowd pressed in, as though the very earth itself longed to hear every word that fell from His lips. I could hear the rustle of cloaks against the grass, sandals shifting on the stones, and the quiet breathing of those pressed shoulder to shoulder across the hillside. Mothers hushed their children, and even the birds seemed to soften their song. Each word He spoke felt like it was meant for me, pulling apart the layers of my soul and laying them bare before God.

He lifted His voice again, and the air seemed to grow heavy with His authority.

"You have heard that our ancestors were told, 'You must not murder. If you commit murder, you are subject to judgment.' But I say, if you are even angry with someone, you are subject to judgment! If you call someone an idiot, you are in danger of being brought before the court. And if you curse someone, you are in danger of the fires of hell.

So if you are presenting a sacrifice at the altar in the Temple, and you suddenly remember that someone has something against you, leave your sacrifice there at the altar. Go and be reconciled to that person. Then come and offer your sacrifice to God.

When you are on the way to court with your adversary, settle your differences quickly. Otherwise, your accuser may hand you over to the judge, who will hand you over to an officer, and you will be thrown into prison. And if that happens, you surely won't be free again until you have paid the last penny."
(Matthew 5:21-26 NLT)

I swallowed hard. His words pierced deeper than any sword. I had not killed, but I knew anger. I had carried it in my heart toward men who had cheated me in business, toward neighbors who had spoken against my family. My wife's eyes glistened as she glanced at me. She too knew the sharp sting of bitterness, the temptation to lash out when wronged.

He wasn't speaking of outward acts alone—He was cutting into the very root of the heart. It was not enough to keep our hands from blood if our hearts seethed with hatred.

I felt a stirring inside—conviction, yes, but also hope. For as much as His words wounded, they also healed. It was as if He was showing us not only who we were, but who we could become.

And before the whispers of the crowd faded, His voice rang out again, strong and unrelenting:

"You have heard the commandment that says, 'You must not commit adultery.' But I say, anyone who even looks at a woman with lust has already committed adultery with her in his heart.

So if your eye—even your good eye—causes you to lust, gouge it out and throw it away. It is better for you to lose one part of your body than for your whole body to be thrown into hell. And if your hand—even your stronger hand—causes you to sin, cut it off and throw it away. It is better for you to lose one part of your body than for your whole body to be thrown into hell."
(Matthew 5:27-30 NLT)

The weight of His words overwhelmed me. I had thought sin was only what could be seen, but here He was uncovering what no one else could see—what lived in the secret places of the heart. My wife trembled beside me, holding our daughter tightly, as though shielding her from a broken world.

I looked out over the multitude—farmers with sun-worn faces, widows with grief carved into their eyes, young men eager yet restless, children squirming on laps. Every soul seemed laid bare. Some bowed their heads in shame, others lifted tear-streaked faces toward heaven. But none could deny the power of His words.

And within me, something unexpected rose—a longing. A longing not just to be free of outward guilt, but to be pure in the very depths of my soul.

I whispered to my wife, my voice trembling, "He speaks as if God sees everything—and yet still calls us to Himself."

She nodded, her tears falling freely now. "This... this is not like the teaching of the rabbis. This is the voice of Heaven."

The hours seemed to slip away as He continued teaching. It wasn't like the rabbis we had heard in the synagogues—dry, rigid, and heavy with burdens no man could bear. This was different. His words were alive, sharp and yet tender, filled with both authority and love. Every sentence seemed to reach into the deepest places of our hearts, exposing what we tried to hide and at the same time healing wounds we thought would never mend.

He taught about anger, reconciliation, purity, marriage, vows, revenge, and love for enemies. Who could speak with such boldness? Who could command the soul with both fire and gentleness? We were amazed, as were the thousands scattered across the hillside that day. It seemed every man, woman, and child sat in stunned silence, unwilling to miss even the sound of His breathing between phrases.

The sun shone warmly on our backs, wrapping us in golden light. A soft breeze swept up the slope, carrying with it the fresh scent of water from the Sea of Galilee. From where we sat, the glimmer of the lake stretched out like a mirror of the heavens, its waves rolling gently in the afternoon light. Fishermen's boats dotted the waters below, their sails like small white birds drifting lazily.

The Sea itself lay cradled in the valley, surrounded by rising hills and fertile plains where wheat and barley grew. Villages were scattered along its shores—Capernaum, Bethsaida, Magdala—each sending people who now sat among us, listening. That same water which sustained life in Galilee now seemed to echo the words of life pouring from His lips.

I looked around at the multitude. Rugged shepherds leaned on their staffs, merchants who had traveled dusty roads sat with their wares beside them, mothers rocked their infants quietly, children clung to their fathers' arms—all stilled by the voice of one Man. Never had we experienced such unity in silence. Not fear, not compulsion, but awe.

I turned slightly toward her, my voice barely more than a whisper. "Do you sense it? Truly, Heaven itself is here with us on this hill." She nodded, her eyes never leaving Him. "He speaks as no one ever has."

The hillside was hushed, the sea below shimmering as if reflecting heaven itself. The warmth of the sun bathed us, and the gentle breeze carried His words across the multitude like a living current. No one stirred—not even the children. It was as though thousands of souls were bound together in a single longing to drink in every word He spoke. He had spoken of anger and purity of heart, and before the weight of those words had even settled, He began again, His voice steady and sure.

"You have heard the law that says, 'A man can divorce his wife by merely giving her a written notice of divorce.' But I say that a man who divorces his wife, unless she has been unfaithful, causes her to commit adultery. And anyone who marries a divorced woman also commits adultery.

You have also heard that our ancestors were told, 'You must not break your vows; you must carry out the vows you make to the Lord.' But I say, do not make any vows! Do not say, 'By heaven!' because heaven is God's throne. And do not say, 'By the earth!' because the earth is his footstool. And do not say, 'By Jerusalem!' for Jerusalem is the city of the great King. Do not even say, 'By my head!' for you can't turn one hair white or black. Just say a simple, 'Yes, I will,' or 'No, I won't.' Anything beyond this is from the evil one." (Matthew 5:31–37 NLT)

I could feel my wife's hand tremble in mine. His words about marriage and vows cut deeply, yet I saw in her eyes a quiet gladness, as though He was guarding the covenant we shared. To think that God Himself valued the bond between husband and wife with such weight—it stirred in me a renewed devotion. And His call to honesty, to let my "yes" be yes and my "no" be no, pierced me. How often had I shaded the truth in business, in casual talk? His words stripped all excuses away.

And then He lifted His voice again, each phrase striking like lightning against the ways of men:

"You have heard the law that says the punishment must match the injury: 'An eye for an eye, and a tooth for a tooth.' But I say, do not resist an evil person! If someone slaps you on the right cheek, offer the other cheek also. If you are sued in court and your shirt is taken from you, give your coat, too. If a soldier demands that you carry his gear for a mile, carry it two miles. Give to those who ask,

and don't turn away from those who want to borrow."
(Matthew 5:38–42 NLT)

The crowd shifted uneasily. These words were unlike any-thing we had ever been taught. In Tyre, in Galilee, in every place I had lived or traded, men took pride in standing their ground, in vengeance, in strength. Yet here He was, speaking of surrender, of giving more than what was demanded. I thought of the Roman sol-diers who so often pressed us into service, their voices harsh, their commands heavy. Could it be possible to willingly go farther than they required? Everything in me recoiled, and yet His words did not feel like weakness—they carried a power I could not explain.

The breeze stirred again, the sound of the waves far below min-gling with His voice as He spoke what seemed the most impossible of all:

"You have heard the law that says, 'Love your neighbor' and hate your enemy. But I say, love your enemies! Pray for those who persecute you! In that way, you will be acting as true children of your Father in heaven. For he gives his sunlight to both the evil and the good, and he sends rain on the just and the unjust alike.

If you love only those who love you, what reward is there for that? Even corrupt tax collectors do that much. If you are kind only to your friends, how are you different from anyone else? Even pagans do that. But you are to be perfect, even as your Father in heaven is perfect." (Matthew 5:43–48 NLT)

My mind raced, torn by the weight of His words. Love your enemies? Pray for those who mock and wound and take from you?

Everything in my flesh wanted to reject it, yet His voice carried such weight that I could not escape. His words did not merely command—they invited. They called me into a life higher, deeper, truer than anything I had ever known.

I glanced at my wife. Tears streamed down her cheeks, but her face was radiant. "This is the way of Heaven," she whispered. "Not just rules—not just words—this is life."

And I knew she was right. For though His teaching broke me, it also remade me. On that hillside, with the Sea of Galilee shimmering below and the sun setting into gold, it felt as though Heaven itself had drawn near.

The sun drifted lower, turning the hillside golden. The breeze off the Sea of Galilee cooled our skin, but inside, our hearts burned hotter with every word He spoke. Never had we heard teaching like this—filled with power, yet drenched in love. It was not the voice of a man quoting traditions; it was as though the very heartbeat of The Kingdom of God was being spoken aloud. Thousands sat on the slope that day, and though we came from villages and cities scattered across the land, we were united—silent, captivated, hanging on every word.

Jesus lifted His eyes, and His voice carried again across the multitude:

"Watch out! Don't do your good deeds publicly, to be admired by others, for you will lose the reward from your Father in heaven. When you give to someone in need, don't do as the hypocrites do—blowing trumpets in the synagogues and streets to call attention to their acts of charity! I tell you the truth, they have received all the reward they will ever get. But when you give to someone in need, don't let your left hand know what your right hand is doing. Give your gifts in private, and your Father, who sees everything, will reward you." (Matthew 6:1–4 NLT)

I thought of the times I had given coins in the marketplace, making sure others had seen. His words stung, but in the sting came freedom. He was not after my display—He was after my heart.

He paused, and then His tone grew even more intimate, like a Father teaching His children:

"When you pray, don't be like the hypocrites who love to pray publicly on street corners and in the synagogues where everyone can see them. I tell you the truth, that is all the reward they will ever get. But when you pray, go away by yourself, shut the door behind you, and pray to your Father in private. Then your Father, who sees everything, will reward you.

When you pray, don't babble on and on as people of other religions do. They think their prayers are answered merely by repeating their words again and again. Don't be like them, for your Father knows exactly what you need even before you ask him! Pray like this:

Our Father in heaven, may your name be kept holy.

May your Kingdom come soon.

May your will be done on earth, as it is in heaven.

Give us today the food we need, and forgive us our sins, as we have forgiven those who sin against us.

And don't let us yield to temptation, but rescue us from the evil one." (Matthew 6:5–13 NLT)

The words sank deep. "Our Father..." Not distant, not unreachable, but near—like the very air we breathed. My wife squeezed my hand, her face wet with tears. "He speaks as though the Almighty Himself welcomes us as children," she whispered.

He went on, piercing deeper still:

"If you forgive those who sin against you, your heavenly Father will forgive you. But if you refuse to forgive others, your Father will not forgive your sins." (Matthew 6:14–15 NLT)

Forgive...? My mind reeled with the faces of men who had wronged me, cheated me, mocked me. To forgive them seemed impossible. Yet when I looked into His face, glowing with the light of heaven, I knew He would never ask what was not possible through God.

The hillside remained utterly silent, the Sea of Galilee shimmering like glass in the distance, boats bobbing gently near its shores. And Jesus continued, His words flowing like a river that could not be stopped—about fasting, about storing up treasures in heaven, about serving God alone, about not worrying what we would eat or wear.

It was overwhelming, and yet every sentence felt like life itself. Each word cut and healed all at once.

The shadows on the hillside stretched long as the sun drifted westward. The Sea of Galilee below glistened with rippling light, its waves rolling softly against the shore. Fishing boats swayed in the breeze, and the scent of the water mingled with the grass on the slope where thousands of us still sat, hearts captured by every word of Jesus. None moved away. None grew weary of listening. It was as though His voice itself gave us strength.

He lifted His eyes toward us again, His tone steady, calling us higher:

"Don't store up treasures here on earth, where moths eat them and rust destroys them, and where thieves break in and steal. Store your treasures in heaven, where moths and rust cannot destroy, and thieves do not break in and steal. Wherever your treasure is, there the desires of your heart will also be.

Your eye is like a lamp that provides light for your body. When your eye is healthy, your whole body is filled with light. But when your eye is unhealthy, your whole body is filled with darkness. And if the light you think you have is actually darkness, how deep that darkness is!

No one can serve two masters. For you will hate one and love the other; you will be devoted to one and despise the other. You cannot serve God and be enslaved to money."
(Matthew 6:19–24 NLT)

His words pierced me. I thought of the coins I had worked so hard to earn in Tyre, of the goods I had traded, of the comfort I longed to provide for my family. All of it could be eaten, rusted, or stolen in a single night. Yet He spoke of a treasure beyond reach of moth or thief. My wife leaned close, her whisper breaking the silence: "Perhaps all along, we've been seeking the wrong wealth."

As though He heard our very thoughts, His next words fell like a balm on our anxious hearts:

"That is why I tell you not to worry about everyday life—whether you have enough food and drink, or enough clothes to wear. Isn't life more than food, and your body more than clothing? Look at the birds. They don't plant or harvest or store food in barns, for your heavenly Father feeds them. And aren't you far more valuable to him than they are? Can all your worries add a single moment to your life?

And why worry about your clothing? Look at the lilies of the field and how they grow. They don't work or make their clothing, yet Solomon in all his glory was not dressed as beautifully as they are. And if God cares so wonderfully for wildflowers that are here today and thrown into the fire tomorrow, he will certainly care for you. Why do you have so little faith?

So don't worry about these things, saying, 'What will we eat? What will we drink? What will we wear?' These things dominate the thoughts of unbelievers, but your heavenly Father already knows all your needs. Seek the Kingdom of God above all else, and live righteously, and he will give you everything you need.

So don't worry about tomorrow, for tomorrow will bring its own worries. Today's trouble is enough for today."
(Matthew 6:25–34 NLT)

Tears blurred my sight as I lifted my eyes over the hillside. Birds darted across the evening sky, their wings glinting in the sun's fading rays. Wildflowers swayed gently in the breeze, simple and beautiful, clothing the earth better than any king. An ache welled deep within me, for I realized how much of my life had been ruled by worry—by wages, by debts, by food and clothing. Yet here He was, speaking as if the God of heaven already saw, already knew, already cared.

My wife pressed our little ones close and whispered through her tears, "If He feeds the birds, He will feed us too. If He clothes the lilies, He will clothe us."

I nodded, my voice unsteady. "And if we seek His Kingdom first, we lack nothing."

All around us, faces glowed with awe. Farmers, fishermen, widows, tax collectors, children—all sat still as if eternity itself rested on these words. And within me, a seed of trust was planted, deeper than fear, deeper than worry.

The sky had begun to soften into hues of amber and rose, the light reflecting off the Sea of Galilee in shimmering bands. Still, not one person moved from the hillside. Thousands remained, eyes fastened on Him, as though each word was bread for our souls. Children leaned against their parents, the weary forgot their hunger, and the skeptical found themselves caught in wonder. He had spoken of treasures, of lilies, of a Father who knew our needs. And before the echoes of those words could fade, He spoke again—cutting deep, yet with a gentleness that drew us closer.

"Do not judge others, and you will not be judged. For you will be treated as you treat others. The standard you use in judging is the standard by which you will be judged.

And why worry about a speck in your friend's eye when you have a log in your own? How can you think of saying to your friend, 'Let me help you get rid of that speck in your eye,' when you can't see past the log in your own eye? Hypocrite! First get rid of the log in your own eye; then you will see well enough to deal with the speck in your friend's eye." (Matthew 7:1–5 NLT)

The crowd shifted uneasily, a few nervous chuckles rising then fading into silence. I felt my wife's hand tighten in mine. I had judged harshly, even in the journey here—judged those who mocked our leaving Tyre, judged neighbors, judged those I thought less holy. His words burned; they left no place for pride. And yet, strangely, they did not condemn. They invited humility, a chance to see myself truly before God.

Before my thoughts could settle, His voice rose again:

"Keep on asking, and you will receive what you ask for. Keep on seeking, and you will find. Keep on knocking, and the door will be opened to you. For everyone who asks, receives. Everyone who seeks, finds. And to everyone who knocks, the door will be opened.

You parents—if your children ask for a loaf of bread, do you give them a stone instead? Or if they ask for a fish, do you give them a snake? Of course not! So if you sinful people know how to give good gifts to your children, how much more will your heavenly Father give good gifts to those who ask him.

Do to others whatever you would like them to do to you. This is the essence of all that is taught in the law and the prophets." (Matthew 7:7–12 NLT)

I looked at my children nestled against their mother, their small hands clutching her robe. I would never deny them bread if they hungered. Could it be true—could the Almighty care for us with even greater love? The thought overwhelmed me. My wife's tears streamed freely as she whispered, "He is not distant. He is a Father."

Jesus' eyes swept over the crowd, and His tone grew urgent, calling us to decision:

"You can enter God's Kingdom only through the narrow gate. The highway to hell is broad, and its gate is wide for the many who choose that way. But the gateway to life is very narrow and the road is difficult, and only a few ever find it." (Matthew 7:13–14 NLT)

The hillside grew still. His words were sobering—life or destruction, no middle ground. I felt the weight press upon my soul. Would we have the courage to walk that narrow road?

And before the crowd could even murmur, He warned us further, His voice steady but filled with urgency:

"Beware of false prophets who come disguised as harmless sheep but are really vicious wolves. You can identify them by their fruit, that is, by the way they act. Can you pick grapes from thornbushes, or figs from thistles? A good tree produces good fruit, and a bad tree produces bad fruit. A good tree can't produce bad fruit, and a bad tree can't produce good fruit. So every tree that does not produce good fruit is chopped down and thrown into the fire. Yes, just as you can identify a tree by its fruit, so you can identify people by their actions.

Not everyone who calls out to me, 'Lord! Lord!' will enter the Kingdom of Heaven. Only those who actually do the will of my Father in heaven will enter. On judgment day many will say to me, 'Lord! Lord! We prophesied in your name and cast out demons in your name and performed many miracles in your name.' But I will reply, 'I never knew you. Get away from me, you who break God's laws.'" (Matthew 7:15–23 NLT)

The weight of His words pressed harder. My wife's hand trembled in mine. To think that even those who spoke His name could be turned away if their lives bore no fruit—it shook me. He was not calling us to empty words or outward shows, but to a life transformed by obedience to the Father's will.

And then, as the wind stirred the tall grasses around us, He spoke of what it meant to truly belong to Him:

"Anyone who listens to my teaching and follows it is wise, like a person who builds a house on solid rock. Though the rain comes in torrents and the floodwaters rise and the winds beat against that house, it won't collapse because it is built on bedrock. But anyone who hears my teaching and doesn't obey it is foolish, like a person who builds a house on sand. When the rains and floods come and the winds beat against that house, it will collapse with a mighty crash." (Matthew 7:24–27 NLT)

His words fell like thunder across my soul. I had built my life on shifting sands—on wages, on reputation, on my own strength. Yet He spoke of a foundation that could not be shaken. My wife turned to me, her eyes blazing with conviction. "We must build on Him," she whispered. "On His words—nothing else will stand."

When He finished, a hush deeper than any I had ever known settled over the hillside. The crowd, thousands strong, sat stunned. Never had we heard anyone teach like this. It was not the echo of traditions, nor the burden of endless rules. It was authority. It was life.

The Sea of Galilee shimmered in the fading light, and as the breeze swept over us, I felt it deep within—He was not just teaching us how to live. He was calling us to Himself.

As the last of His words settled like a holy fire across the hillside, silence lingered. It was the kind of silence that carried weight—thousands of people, yet no one dared to speak too quickly. The Sea of Galilee glistened in the fading light below, waves lapping gently at the shore as though creation itself was bowing to the Word spoken among us.

Then, slowly, the crowd began to stir. Mothers lifted their children, fathers rose to their feet, the elderly leaned on staffs as they carefully stood. Yet no one hurried away. It was as though all of us carried something fragile and holy, something we dared not let slip away in idle chatter.

I held my wife's hand as we began to walk down the slope with our little ones beside us. She turned to me, her voice hushed, "I feel as if my heart has been lit aflame—and it will never be the same."

I nodded, the weight of His words still pressing into me. "I thought we came to find a teacher," I said softly, "but what we found was more than a teacher. He speaks with the authority of Heaven."

Around us, people murmured with the same awe. A fisherman marveled aloud, "Never have I heard such words—not from scribes, not from priests. He speaks, and it is as though God Himself is among us." Another man, a shepherd by the look of his cloak, shook his head in wonder. "When He spoke of building on the rock, I felt it—my life has been nothing but shifting sand."

Everywhere I looked, faces were radiant, some streaked with tears, others alight with hope. It was as if the very air was alive, carrying His words within it still.

As we reached the base of the hill, the crowd pressed closer, for Jesus Himself was now descending, His disciples near Him. The multitude did not scatter as they might after a rabbi's teaching—they followed. Men, women, children, rich and poor, broken and whole—all drawn as if by an unseen hand.

And as He reached the bottom, a man afflicted with leprosy came forward. The crowd gasped, drawing back in fear, for no one dared come near the unclean. Yet the man fell on his knees before Jesus, his voice trembling: "Lord, if you are willing, you can heal me and make me clean."

We held our children close, scarcely able to breathe. What would He do?

Jesus stepped forward—closer, not away. He reached out His hand and touched the man. Touched him! The crowd inhaled sharply. And Jesus spoke with the same authority that had burned in our hearts all day: "I am willing. Be healed!"

In an instant, the leper's skin was restored, clean and whole. A cry of awe and joy erupted from the multitude. My wife pressed her hands to her mouth, tears flowing freely. I could only whisper, "Truly, the Kingdom of God has come near."

And in that moment, I knew the journey from Tyre, the wages lost, the risks taken—all of it was worth it. We had found Him. And nothing would ever be the same.

That evening we found a place to rest along the edge of the town, where many of the crowd also lingered. Some returned to their villages, but many, like us, could not bear to leave just yet. The sun had slipped behind the hills, painting the horizon in deep purples and gold, and the air carried the cool scent of the Sea of Galilee as the night settled.

We spread a small blanket on the ground and shared the bread we had carried from Tyre, though none of us were truly hungry. My mind was too full, my heart too stirred to think of food. Our children nibbled quietly, their eyes wide as they whispered about what they had seen.

"Did you see Him touch the man with the sickness?" my daughter asked, her voice hushed, as though speaking too loudly might break the holiness of the moment.

"Yes," my wife answered, brushing a hand gently over her hair. "And did you see what happened when He touched him? The sickness was gone. Just like that."

Our son leaned forward, his eyes shining in the firelight from a nearby family. "He wasn't afraid, not even of the leprosy."

I looked at them, at the innocence in their faces, and my heart ached with both wonder and longing. "Children," I said softly, "we heard words today that no one has ever spoken before. Words about love, forgiveness, and the Kingdom of Heaven. And now, we have seen with our own eyes that His words carry power. He does not just speak—He does what no one else can do."

My wife's gaze met mine across the dim light. "He spoke of a Father in heaven who knows our needs," she whispered, her voice trembling. "I have never thought of God that way—so near, so tender, as a Father who loves His children."

I nodded, feeling tears well up again. "And He called us to trust, not to worry. To love, even our enemies. To build our lives on His words as on solid rock. What else can we do but follow Him?"

The children leaned against us, their eyes heavy with sleep, but I knew the memory of the day was etched into their hearts as deeply as it was into ours. We lay beneath the stars, listening to the gentle lapping of the sea on the shore, our thoughts still filled with His voice, His face, His touch upon the leper.

As my eyes closed, one thought remained: we had come searching for a man spoken of in whispers. What we found was more than a man. We had found the One who carried Heaven in His voice and life in His hands.

Scriptures: Matthew chapters 5, 6 and 7 and Luke 6:17–49

The Centurion

I WAS A SOLDIER of Rome. Discipline, loyalty, and obedience were the air I breathed. My life was measured in orders given and orders carried out, in strength and control. To lead men, you had to be firm, unbending. Love had little place in the world I knew.

But then I encountered Him—Jesus of Nazareth.

At first, I stood at the edge of the crowds. I watched Him from a distance, not wanting to be noticed. I had seen kings and governors, men who held armies at their command, but this man held something far greater. He spoke, and the people hung on every word as though His words were life itself. He touched the broken, and they were made whole. He lifted the heads of the outcast with a tenderness I had never seen. His authority was undeniable, but it was wrapped in something Rome could never understand—love.

That love disarmed me. It reached places in me I did not even know were wounded. With every teaching, every miracle, every act of mercy, my heart shifted. I had seen rulers use fear to bend men, but Jesus used compassion to draw them. And not just the Jews—He welcomed even Gentiles like me.

The day my servant fell ill was the day my heart was torn open. To others he was only a servant, but to me he was like the very breath of my own household—a son of my heart, though not of my blood. I still remember the first time I saw him, a frail boy with eyes too weary for his age. I could not leave him to the cruelty of the streets, so I brought him under my roof. Through the years, he grew strong and steady, faithful in every task, yet it was his gentle spirit that marked him most. He brought life to my home, joy to those around him, and comfort to me in my loneliest hours.

When sickness gripped him, all the strength of Rome in my command meant nothing. I would have faced a thousand enemies on the battlefield rather than watch him suffer a single day. Each breath he struggled for cut into me like a blade. Death drew near, and for the first time in all my years as a soldier, I felt powerless. My heart broke at the thought of losing him, for he was not simply in my care—he was part of me.

And then—Jesus.

I believed He could heal him. No, more than believed—I was convinced. But I could not bring myself to ask Him to enter my home. Who was I? A soldier of Rome, unworthy of the presence of such holiness. My sins, my failures, my bloodied hands—I could not bring that into His shadow.

I came to Him, a storm of desperation pushing me forward. My servant—my son in all but blood—lay at the edge of death. When I saw Jesus, hope stirred where despair had nearly drowned me.

"Lord," I said, my voice trembling though I was a soldier used to command, "my servant lies at home, paralyzed and in terrible suffering."

At once He answered, "I will come and heal him."

But I could not let Him. My knees nearly gave way as I spoke, "Lord, I am not worthy to have You enter my home. Just speak the word from where You stand, and my servant will be healed."

I looked into His eyes and felt as though He saw the very depths of me. "I know authority," I continued. "I am under my commanders, and I myself have soldiers under me. I say 'Go,' and they go; 'Come,' and they come. I tell my servant, 'Do this,' and he does it. If such power rests in me under Rome, how much more is in You? You carry authority not only over men, but over sickness, over spirits, over life itself."

In that moment, silence seemed to stretch across the crowd. Then Jesus turned, and with wonder in His voice said to those around us, "I tell you the truth, I haven't seen faith like this in all Israel!"

The words struck me like a blessing poured from Heaven. The Son of God, marveling at me—a foreigner, a Roman. My eyes burned with tears I could not hold back. His love, His authority, His very presence was greater than anything I had ever known. And I knew, even before I turned back toward home, that my servant was already healed.

I left Jesus with His words echoing in my soul. Each step back toward my house felt like a battle between fear and faith. The world seemed to still as I turned the final corner, every step carrying the gravity of His promise.

Servants rushed out to meet me before I even crossed the threshold. Their faces shone with wonder. "Master!" one cried, his voice shaking, "he is well—completely well! The fever left him at once."

I pushed past them and into the room where he had been lying. My servant—my son in every way that mattered—stood there, strength restored, color returned to his face. He looked at me with tears streaming down his cheeks, and before I could stop myself, I embraced him. For all my years as a soldier, hardened by blood and battle, I wept openly.

"When?" I managed to ask, pulling back to see his eyes.

They told me the very hour the fever broke. My knees went weak as I realized—it was the very hour I stood before Jesus and heard Him marvel at my faith.

In that moment, my life was no longer my own. All the power of Rome, all the victories of my sword, meant nothing beside the authority and love of this Man. My servant lived because Jesus spoke life. And I knew, as surely as I knew my own name, that He was no mere teacher. He was Lord over all.

Looking back now, I see that day as the turning point of my life. For three years, I had listened at the edges of crowds, my heart softened bit by bit by His words. That day, it was completed. I no longer only admired Him; I believed with all my heart. Jesus was not just a healer. He was the Messiah, the Son of God.

And I knew then—His love was not only strong enough to heal the sick. His love was strong enough to heal hardened hearts like mine.

Scriptures: Luke 7:1–9, Matthew 8:5–13

Widow's Son

THE DAY HAD BEEN heavy with silence. My son—my only son—was gone. The house felt empty, stripped of laughter and warmth, and my heart seemed hollow, as though it had been carved out of me. I walked beside his body, wrapped in linen, carried out of the town. The wailing of those around me rose into the air, but inside I was numb. I had already buried my husband years before. Now my boy, the last piece of my life, the one who should have carried on our family name, was gone too.

The procession moved slowly through the narrow street, the sound of sandals dragging against the dirt mingling with muffled sobs and the sharp wail of mourners. The air was heavy, thick with the scent of burning oil lamps and the bitter spices used to cover death's sting. Dust clung to our skin and mixed with the salt of our tears, leaving a dryness in my mouth I could not swallow away. I heard the low murmur of neighbors, their voices hushed with sorrow, yet above it all was the silence of my son—no laughter, no words, only stillness wrapped in linen. Every step forward felt like it carried me deeper into a darkness I could not escape.

Each step felt like I was being pulled further into darkness. People said words meant to comfort, but their voices could not reach the ache inside me. I looked at his still face and whispered in my heart, "Why, Lord? Why must I walk this road alone?"

As we came near the town gate, I lifted my eyes for a moment—and I saw Him. A crowd followed Him, their faces alight with something I hadn't seen in years: hope. He looked at me, and in that single glance I felt the weight of my sorrow uncovered. It was as though He saw not only the tears streaming down my face but the years of loneliness and pain etched deep within me.

Then He spoke, His voice gentle yet full of authority: "Don't cry." How could I not? Yet something in His words pressed into the deepest part of me.

He stepped forward and placed His hand on the wooden frame where my son's body lay. The men carrying my son stopped. Time itself seemed to halt. I could hardly breathe. Then He said words that shattered the silence: 'Young man, I tell you, get up.'

I gasped as I saw my son's chest rise with breath. His eyes opened. He sat up and began to speak. My trembling hands reached for him, tears flooding down my face, but this time they were not tears of sorrow—they were tears of life. Jesus gave him back to me.

The crowd erupted, voices crying out in awe, "A mighty prophet has risen among us!" and "God has visited His people today!" But for me, all the world faded away. My son was alive, in my arms again.

I could hardly speak. My heart, once buried in grief, now overflowed with a joy I could not contain. In that moment, I knew I had been seen by God, held by His mercy. My life, once emptied, was filled again.

Scriptures: Luke 7:11-17

My Hand

FOR AS LONG AS I can remember, my right hand had been useless—twisted, shriveled, a constant reminder of my brokenness. It wasn't just the physical pain or the awkward stares that weighed on me, but the deep ache of not being able to provide as other men did. In our world, a man's strength was his work, his honor. Without it, I was often overlooked, pitied, even judged. Some whispered that perhaps I had sinned, that my affliction was a punishment from God. Every day, I carried that shame like a cloak.

Still, I went to the synagogue. I wanted to worship, to hear the Scriptures, to keep my hope alive. That Sabbath morning felt no different as I entered and found my place along the wall. But in the air there was something heavy, something charged. Jesus was there.

By then, everyone knew His name. He had healed the sick, cast out demons, even touched lepers without fear. Some whispered He might be the Messiah. Others said He was dangerous, a deceiver. Wherever He went, the crowds pressed in—and wherever He went, the Pharisees were never far behind.

The Pharisees were the guardians of the Law, or so they thought. They prided themselves on keeping every command, every tradition. They had confronted Jesus before, enraged that His disciples picked grain on the Sabbath, angry that He ate with sinners and tax collectors, offended by His authority when He spoke of forgiveness. Again and again, they bristled as His words exposed their pride and their blindness. And now, they were here, watching closely, hoping to trap Him.

It didn't take long. His eyes found me. That look—it wasn't pity, but compassion, deep and searching. My whole being tensed as He spoke, "Come and stand in front of everyone."

Every eye in the room turned to me. My legs felt heavy, but I obeyed, stepping into the center where my deformity was laid bare for all to see. Silence wrapped the synagogue, and a thrill of awe surged through me.

Then He spoke—not to me, but to them: "Does the law permit good deeds on the Sabbath, or is it a day for doing evil? Is this a day to save life or to destroy it?"

The question hung in the air like a sword. No one answered. The Pharisees stared, lips pressed tight, unwilling to admit the truth.

I saw the anger rise in Jesus then—holy, righteous anger—not against me, but against the hardness of their hearts. And with it, sorrow. He longed for them to see, to believe, to rejoice in the goodness of God. Yet their blindness was complete.

Then He turned back to me. His voice was steady, filled with authority. "Stretch out your hand."

My mind raced. That hand had brought me only shame and ridicule. It was the part of me I wished to hide, not expose. But His words carried a power I couldn't resist. With trembling faith, I stretched it out.

And in that instant, life surged through it. Warmth, strength, wholeness—like fire and water all at once. Before my very eyes, my twisted fingers uncurled, my shriveled muscles filled out, my skin grew firm and strong. My hand was restored—completely, perfectly—like the other.

Gasps filled the room. A murmur spread through the crowd. Some whispered in awe, others covered their mouths in wonder. I flexed my hand again and again, tears streaming down my face. For the first time in years, I could feel the strength in my grip. I could work, I could provide, I could embrace my children with both arms.

But not everyone rejoiced.

I looked to the Pharisees, hoping they too might be moved, that they might see the hand of God revealed. Instead, I saw fury. Their jaws clenched, their eyes blazed, and their silence was thick with rage. To them, it didn't matter that a broken man had been made whole. All they could see was that Jesus had done it on the Sabbath.

In their hearts, mercy had no place—only law. Compassion had no weight—only ritual. They valued control above truth, their traditions above the Kingdom of God. They had witnessed a miracle of life, yet they hardened themselves against it.

I watched as they turned sharply, their robes sweeping the floor as they stormed toward the doorway. Their whispers were sharp, venomous. They spoke not of worship, not of awe, but of schemes. They were already plotting how to rid themselves of Him, how to kill the very One who had come to heal, to save, to set free.

The contrast seared into my soul. My hand, once lifeless, now pulsed with vitality—while their hearts, though outwardly appearing strong, were withered and dead. The same miracle that gave me hope pushed them deeper into hatred. The Savior stood in their midst, but they could not see Him. The Kingdom of God had broken into the room, yet they walked away blind.

That day marked a turning point in my life. For me, it was the beginning of restoration—not only of my hand, but of my hope, my faith, my very life. I would never be the same.

For them, it was the beginning of their plot—the day they resolved not to bow, but to kill the One who brought salvation to all who believe.

I have never forgotten the dividing line of that Sabbath: one broken man made whole, and the keepers of the Law proving to be more broken than they dared to admit.

Scriptures: Matthew 12:9-13, Mark 3:1-6, and Luke 6:6-11

The Seed

I GREW UP IN Cana of Galilee, a farming town tucked in the hills, where the rhythm of life was marked by the soil. My father was a farmer, and from the time I could walk, I followed him into the fields. I learned to read the clouds, to watch the winds, to feel the soil in my hands. The smell of freshly turned earth, the ache of bent knees pulling thorns, the relief of rain after long dryness—these things shaped me.

I knew the joy of good harvest years, when the barns filled and neighbors rejoiced together. And I knew the despair of bad years, when flocks of birds stripped the seed, or the sun scorched shallow roots, or weeds choked out tender plants. Farming taught me that life was fragile, survival uncertain, and every seed mattered.

That's why, the day Jesus stepped into a boat along the Sea of Galilee and began to speak, His words pierced me more than most. He began, "Listen! A farmer went out to plant some seed..."

I glanced at Philip, standing beside me. He smiled faintly and nudged my shoulder. "He's speaking your trade, Bartholomew," he whispered.

And truly, He was.

I was drawn in at once. He was speaking my language. He told of seed falling on a footpath, eaten by birds. Of seed on rocky soil, springing up fast but withering in the sun. Of seed among thorns, smothered and strangled. And finally, of seed on good soil—producing thirty, sixty, even a hundred times what had been planted.

The crowd stirred. Some nodded, others frowned in confusion. But I stood frozen, my heart pounding. I knew every scene He described. I had lived them. Yet I felt He was speaking beyond farming. He was speaking of us.

Later, when we were alone, we asked Him about it. Peter was the first to speak, as usual. "Rabbi," he said, "why do you tell the crowds these stories? Why not just say plainly what you mean?"

Jesus looked at us—His eyes patient, yet searching. "You are permitted to understand the secrets of the Kingdom of God," He said softly. "But others are not. That's why I speak in parables. For those who truly listen, more will be given. But for those who harden their hearts, even what little they think they have will slip away."

His words stirred unease among us. I thought of the prophets, of how Israel had heard God's words for centuries and yet so often turned deaf. Could I also be deaf, blind, hard-hearted?

Andrew leaned closer. "Then tell us, Lord. What did you mean about the farmer and the seed?"

Jesus' face grew intent. "The seed is the word of God," He said. He paused, letting it settle. "Some seed falls on the footpath. That is like people who hear the word, but before it can take root, the devil comes and snatches it away from their hearts. They never believe."

I pictured flocks of birds devouring seed before it ever had a chance. My stomach tightened.

"Other seed falls on rocky ground," He went on. "That is like those who receive the message with joy, but their faith is shallow. When trouble or persecution comes, they quickly fall away because they have no roots."

I remembered shallow patches of earth, plants sprouting quickly and dying just as fast. I thought of men I knew—quick to celebrate God's promises, but vanishing when hardship came.

Then His gaze sharpened. "Other seed falls among thorns. These are those who hear God's word, but their hearts are crowded—by worries, the lure of riches, the pleasures of this life. The message is choked, and no fruit ever comes."

I felt exposed. I knew how the cares of farming, family, money, and fear could weigh on a man. How easy it was to let those things strangle faith.

Finally, His tone lifted with hope. "But the seed that falls on good soil—those are the ones with honest, good hearts. They hear God's word, cling to it, and with patience, they produce a harvest—a crop thirty, sixty, even a hundred times what was planted."

His words hung in the air, heavy and alive. No one spoke for a while. Each of us wrestled in silence.

I thought of my father's fields, of the years spent clearing rocks, pulling weeds, breaking the soil open season after season. I realized then—it wasn't easy to become good soil. It took work. It took surrender. It took breaking and softening.

And I thought of my own heart. Which kind of soil was I? Would His words take root in me, deep and lasting? Or would they be stolen, withered, choked?

That night, lying under the stars, I could still hear His voice. "Anyone with ears to hear should listen and understand." I prayed that my ears would stay open, and my heart would be good soil for His seed.

I still remember walking behind my father as he guided the plow. I was just a boy then, my hands too small to hold the reins, but he let me follow in the furrows he carved through the soil of Cana. The oxen strained, their hooves pressing deep, as the iron blade cut the earth open. The smell of fresh-turned soil filled the air, rich and damp.

My father would pause, leaning on the plow, and say, "Son, good soil doesn't happen by itself. You have to work it. You must break it open, season after season, pull out the stones, burn away the thorns. If you don't, nothing worth keeping will ever grow."

As a child, I didn't grasp the weight of his words. I thought he was just talking about fields, about grain and figs and olives. But standing there with Jesus, hearing His parable and watching it come alive all around us, I realized my father had been speaking a truth far greater than farming.

Good soil was not just land—it was the heart.

When Jesus spoke of the footpath, I remembered patches of earth beaten hard by footsteps and hooves, where seed never had a chance to sink in. My father would shake his head and say, "Nothing grows there until the plow breaks it." And I thought of hardened hearts, unwilling to be broken open by God.

When Jesus spoke of rocky soil, I remembered digging stones from the ground year after year. My father would mutter, "The roots won't go deep if the stones remain." And I thought of those who received God's word with joy but gave up at the first trial, because their faith had no roots.

When He spoke of thorns, I could almost feel them tearing my hands as a boy. I hated thorns—they grew fast, spread wide, and strangled anything good. My father would burn them in heaps, warning me, "If you don't destroy them, they'll destroy your crop." And I thought of the worries, riches, and pleasures of life choking out God's truth before it could grow strong.

But when Jesus spoke of good soil, I remembered harvest days—our family gathering, neighbors singing, the barns filled beyond measure. My father would smile, sweat streaking his face, and say, "This is what we labored for. This is the reward." And I thought of lives that received God's word, clung to it, endured with patience, and bore fruit—thirty, sixty, a hundred times as much.

As these memories stirred, I realized something: all along, God had been preparing me through the soil of Cana to understand the soil of the heart. My father's plow had taught me what Jesus' words now confirmed—the harvest never comes by accident. The soil must be worked, broken, softened. And so must the soul.

I lifted my eyes toward the stars that night and prayed, "Lord, let me be good soil. Turn me over. Break me open. Pull out the stones. Burn away the thorns. Let Your word grow deep in me, and let my life bear fruit for Your Kingdom."

Scriptures: Matthew 13:3-23, Mark 4:1-20, and Luke 8:4-15

The Kingdom

BARTHOLOMEW AND I STAYED back for a moment as the crowd settled. The story of the sower still pressed on our hearts. He broke the silence first.

"Matthew, that teaching..." He shook his head. "The same seed, yet such different soil. Some thriving, some dying."

I looked down at the dust under my feet. "Yes. The Word never changes. But our hearts... they do. I can't help but wonder—what kind of soil am I? For years I was thorny ground, consumed by coins and comfort. And yet... He sowed again, and this time, somehow, it took root."

Before Bartholomew could answer, Jesus lifted His voice once more, and the people hushed.

"Here is another story Jesus told: 'The Kingdom of Heaven is like a farmer who planted good seed in his field. But that night as the workers slept, his enemy came and planted weeds among the wheat, then slipped away. When the crop began to grow and produce grain, the weeds also grew.'" (Matthew 13:24–26 NLT)

I pictured it clearly: green shoots pushing through soil, hope rising with them, only to find weeds twisting around their stalks. My gut tightened. Why wouldn't the farmer rip them out?

Jesus continued: "'The farmer's workers went to him and said, "Sir, the field where you planted that good seed is full of weeds! Where did they come from?" "An enemy has done this!" the farmer exclaimed. "Should we pull out the weeds?" they asked. "No," he replied, "you'll uproot the wheat if you do. Let both grow together until the harvest. Then I will tell the harvesters to sort out the weeds, tie them into bundles, and burn them, and to put the wheat in the barn."'" (Matthew 13:27–30 NLT)

I shivered. Evil would remain for now. The Kingdom was here, but not complete. Patience... always patience with God.

Jesus spoke again: "Here is another illustration Jesus used: 'The Kingdom of Heaven is like a mustard seed planted in a field. It is the smallest of all seeds, but it becomes the largest of garden plants; it grows into a tree, and birds come and make nests in its branches.'" (Matthew 13:31–32 NLT)

Bartholomew leaned toward me and whispered with a grin, "A kingdom, starting from the tiniest seed?"

I smiled back. "Yes. But look at what it becomes. That's His way." And something inside me swelled with hope. We were so few, so ordinary, but this Kingdom—this Kingdom would stretch far beyond us.

Then He gave another picture: "Jesus also used this illustration: 'The Kingdom of Heaven is like the yeast a woman used

in making bread. Even though she put only a little yeast in three measures of flour, it permeated every part of the dough.'"
(Matthew 13:33 NLT)

I closed my eyes and saw my mother kneading dough, just a pinch of yeast spread through the whole batch. That was the Kingdom—quiet, unseen, but transforming everything it touched. That was what His Word was doing in me.

When the crowd left and we gathered in the house, our questions poured out.

"Please explain to us the story of the weeds in the field," I asked.

Jesus answered, "'The Son of Man is the farmer who plants the good seed. The field is the world, and the good seed represents the people of the Kingdom. The weeds are the people who belong to the evil one. The enemy who planted the weeds among the wheat is the devil. The harvest is the end of the world, and the harvesters are the angels.'" (Matthew 13:37–39 NLT)

The room fell silent. A heavy weight settled over me as He continued: "'Just as the weeds are sorted out and burned in the fire, so it will be at the end of the world. The Son of Man will send his angels, and they will remove from his Kingdom everything that causes sin and all who do evil. And the angels will throw them into the fiery furnace, where there will be weeping and gnashing of teeth. Then the righteous will shine like the sun in their Father's Kingdom. Anyone with ears to hear should listen and understand!'"
(Matthew 13:40–43 NLT)

I swallowed hard. The Kingdom was not only treasure—it was truth and judgment. It was light and fire. And His words... they were not suggestions. They were reality.

But then His tone softened: "'The Kingdom of Heaven is like a treasure that a man discovered hidden in a field. In his excitement, he hid it again and sold everything he owned to get enough money to buy the field. Again, the Kingdom of Heaven is like a merchant on the lookout for choice pearls. When he discovered a pearl of great value, he sold everything he owned and bought it!'" (Matthew 13:44–46 NLT)

Tears blurred my eyes. That was me. I had left my booth, my coins, my reputation. Why? Because I had found a greater treasure. And I would do it all again.

Jesus lifted His voice once more: "'Again, the Kingdom of Heaven is like a fishing net that was thrown into the water and caught fish of every kind. When the net was full, they dragged it up onto the shore, sat down, and sorted the good fish into crates, but threw the bad ones away. That is the way it will be at the end of the world. The angels will come and separate the wicked people from the righteous, throwing the wicked into the fiery furnace, where there will be weeping and gnashing of teeth.'" (Matthew 13:47–50 NLT)

I thought of the fishermen among us, their nets heavy with the day's catch, straining to separate the good from the bad. That was the Kingdom too: not only growth and treasure, but also final separation.

Then He looked at us, His eyes searching. "'Do you understand all these things?'"

"Yes," we replied. And though I knew my understanding was still dim, something inside me had shifted.

"Then he added, 'Every teacher of religious law who becomes a disciple in the Kingdom of Heaven is like a homeowner who brings from his storeroom new gems of truth as well as old.'" (Matthew 13:51–52 NLT)

I thought of the Law, the Prophets, the promises of old. Now I saw them shining with new light in Him. Old treasures, yes—but new ones too, more radiant than I had ever known.

As the sun sank low, stretching long shadows across the fields, my heart whispered a prayer: "Lord, let me see Your Kingdom as You see it. Let me treasure it above all else. Make me soil where Your seed will grow and bear fruit that lasts."

Scriptures: Matthew 13:24-52

Sea of Galilee

THE DAY HAD BEEN long, the crowds pressing in on every side as Jesus taught beside the lake. My brother John and I had been close to Him since the beginning, yet every time He spoke, it was as if heaven itself broke open before us. That evening, when the sun hung low and the light danced like gold across the Sea of Galilee, Jesus turned to us and said, "Let's cross to the other side of the lake."

John nudged me with his elbow. "James, this is our kind of work," he whispered with a grin.

We didn't hesitate. Boats were our life—we grew up on these waters. The gentle rhythm of waves and the scent of wet nets were familiar to us. Leaving the crowd behind, several of us disciples pushed off, the boat rocking gently as the sails caught the breeze. Jesus, weary from the day, settled down in the back with His head on a cushion. In moments, He was asleep.

At first, the night seemed calm, the lake reflecting the fading light of the sky. But Galilee can turn in an instant. I had seen storms rise here before, but this one—this was like no other. The wind screamed down from the mountains, fierce and merciless, and the waves rose up like dark walls around us. Water slammed into the boat, filling it faster than we could bail.

Fear tore through me. I knew boats. I knew storms. But this one had death in it. My hands shook as I gripped the side, drenched to the bone, salt and spray burning my eyes. I glanced at John—his face was pale, his strength spent as we struggled to keep the vessel from splitting apart.

And all the while—Jesus slept.

Finally, with a desperation I had never known, I stumbled to Him, shaking Him awake. "Teacher, don't you care that we're going to drown?" My voice cracked, choked by fear.

He rose, calm and steady, His eyes filled not with panic, but authority. He looked out at the chaos around us—wind shrieking, waves crashing—and with a voice that cut through the storm, He commanded, "Silence! Be still!"

At once the wind stopped. The sea, which moments before had raged like a beast, grew calm as glass. The storm that had nearly swallowed us was gone, as if it had never been.

Then His gaze turned to us—piercing, gentle, yet firm. "Why are you afraid? Do you still have no faith?"

Those words burned into my heart. It wasn't a passing question; it demanded an answer. He looked at us with an expectancy—as if He truly believed we should have had faith in that moment, that we should have known Him well enough by now to trust Him. And yet, all we had in the storm was fear.

As the boat drifted across the now-still waters, we sat together in silence, glancing at one another. Finally, whispers broke out among the twelve.

Andrew's voice cracked the silence: "Who is this man?"

Peter shook his head slowly, his eyes wide. "Even the wind... and the waves... they obey Him."

Matthew leaned forward, whispering, "I've seen kings and rulers give orders—but creation itself? Who can command that?"

John's voice was hushed, almost trembling: "It's as if the sea itself knows His voice."

I listened to them, my heart pounding so hard I thought it might burst. These were the same waters John and I had fished since we were boys, waters that never bent to any man. We knew how powerless we were when storms came; we had buried friends who didn't make it home. And yet tonight, the sea stilled at His word. Not at ours, not by our strength—but His alone.

I thought of His question again, echoing inside me: "Do you still have no faith?" It cut deep. I wanted to believe I had faith. I wanted to believe I knew Him. But truthfully, I realized I was only beginning. We all were. Sitting there in that quiet boat, the spray drying on my skin, I knew the journey ahead was not just across this lake, but into truly knowing who Jesus is.

Scripture: Mark 4:35–41

The Herdsman

THE HILLS OF THE Decapolis were my home. Our land—ten Greek-influenced cities scattered across this side of the Sea of Galilee—was a place where cultures clashed and overlapped. Rome ruled us, Greeks filled our markets with their gods and customs, and we Jews tried to hold to the Law of Moses. Yet many of us had grown accustomed to compromise.

That was why I tended pigs. To the devout, it was shameful—swine were unclean, forbidden by the Law. But Gentiles in the Decapolis prized them, and Roman soldiers loved their pork. There was money in it, and for many families like mine, survival often outweighed purity. We herdsmen kept watch over the animals day and night, making sure they didn't stray, driving them to pasture, protecting them from thieves, wolves, or storms. It was hard work, not honorable, but it fed our children.

Still, there was something darker in these hills than wolves. The man who haunted the tombs.

Everyone in the region knew him. He had once belonged to our town, but years ago something seized him—an evil no one could name. His madness grew until chains could not restrain him.

We tried, more than once. I had seen strong men bind him with iron shackles, only to watch him snap them like dry reeds. Naked, bloodied from cutting himself with sharp stones, he roamed the tombs screaming into the night. We avoided the road by the caves. Mothers held children close when his howls carried across the valley. He was more beast than man, and yet, in his face, I still saw the shadow of who he once was.

That morning began as any other. My herd grazed near the slope leading down to the sea, the sun just climbing over the eastern ridges. Then I saw a small boat push ashore. A group of men climbed out, led by one whose presence struck me even at a distance. He walked with quiet strength, as though the land itself recognized Him.

Before I could wonder who He was, the wild man appeared—running from the tombs, shrieking. Fear gripped me. Surely, he would attack them. Instead, to my shock, he fell at the feet of the stranger, crying out in a voice that was not his own:

"Why are you interfering with me, Jesus, Son of the Most High God? In the name of God, I beg you, don't torture me!"

Jesus. The name hung in the air like thunder. My pigs stirred nervously.

The man convulsed, the voices within him raging. Jesus commanded them with authority I had never seen: "Come out of the man, you evil spirit!"

The reply was terrifying. "My name is Legion, because there are many of us inside this man. Don't send us far away! Send us into those pigs!"

My heart dropped. Into my herd? Before I could think, Jesus gave them permission.

What followed is seared into me forever. The man screamed as the demons left him. At that instant, my pigs squealed in terror, a sound so piercing it split the air. Two thousand animals surged as one, hooves thundering, eyes wild with panic. I shouted, waved my staff, but they rushed headlong down the slope. The earth shook beneath their weight as they hurled themselves into the sea. Water churned with bodies, foam and squeals filling the air until, in a sickening stillness, it was over. My herd was gone.

I fell to my knees, stunned. My livelihood—years of labor—swept away in a single moment. Yet when I turned back, my anger faltered.

The man—the one who had been a terror to us all—was sitting calmly at Jesus' feet. He was clothed. His face was serene. His eyes, once wild and burning, now shone with clarity, like a man waking from a nightmare. Peace radiated from him. He was whole again.

We herdsmen fled into town, breathless, telling anyone who would listen. Soon the whole countryside came to see. They, too, saw him—the man once possessed, sitting in his right mind—and they trembled with fear. Instead of rejoicing, they begged Jesus to leave. Maybe it was the pigs, maybe it was His power—but they could not bear His presence.

As Jesus turned back to the boat, the restored man pleaded, "Let me go with You!"

But Jesus said, "No, go home to your family, and tell them everything the Lord has done for you and how merciful He has been."

So he obeyed. I saw him later, walking back toward the Decapolis. His steps were steady, his face alive with hope. Soon, reports spread from city to city: the man who once lived among the tombs now spoke openly of the One who delivered him. People marveled, for no one could deny the change.

I lost my herd that day, but I saw something far greater. A man once trapped in darkness was set free, and through the testimony of his life, many would come to know the mercy of God.

Scriptures: Mark 5:1-20

The Alabaster Jar

I'LL NEVER FORGET THAT day.

It was supposed to be a respectable dinner—a polished gathering at the home of Simon the Pharisee. Everything about it felt stiff and religious. Jesus had been invited, and people had gathered mostly out of curiosity. I was there, standing near the wall, trying to stay quiet and out of the way. That's when she came in.

She wasn't invited. And she definitely wasn't welcome.

People recognized her immediately. An immoral woman. A prostitute. Her presence in that room was offensive to almost everyone there. I watched her closely. She walked in trembling, but with a strange determination. In her hands she held an alabaster jar. It was beautiful—carved stone, sealed perfume. Worth a fortune.

And I remember thinking, Why does she have something like that?

Maybe it was the only beautiful thing she had ever owned. Maybe it was something she had saved for years. Maybe it was her way of remembering she still had value, even if the world said otherwise. Whatever it meant to her, it was clear—this jar wasn't just perfume. It was her heart.

She fell to the ground at Jesus' feet.

Then everything seemed to stop.

She wept—not quietly, not politely. Her sobs were deep and aching, years of pain and regret pouring out of her like a flood. Her tears soaked His feet. And without a word, she let down her hair—something a woman never did in public—and used it to wipe His feet clean.

Then, she broke the jar.

The scent exploded through the room—rich, unmistakable, overwhelming. And she poured it out—all of it. Her treasure. Her story. Her shame. Her worship.

You could hear the murmurs rising. The disgust. The judgment. And that's when Jesus spoke.

He turned toward Simon, His host, and said, "Simon, I have something to say to you."

Simon answered politely, "Go ahead, Teacher."

Jesus told a story: "A man loaned money to two people—500 pieces of silver to one, and 50 to the other. But neither of them could repay him, so he kindly forgave them both, canceling their debts. Who do you suppose loved him more after that?"

Simon shifted a little. You could tell he knew it was a setup. Still, he answered, "I suppose the one who had the bigger debt forgiven."

Jesus smiled slightly. "You have judged correctly."

Then He turned and looked at the woman. And still speaking to Simon, He said, "Do you see this woman?"

Do you see her?

He went on: "When I entered your home, you didn't offer me water to wash the dust from my feet, but she has washed them with her tears and wiped them with her hair. You didn't greet me with a kiss, but from the time I came in, she hasn't stopped kissing my feet. You neglected the courtesy of olive oil to anoint my head, but she has anointed my feet with rare perfume."

And then He said the words I'll never forget:

"I tell you, her sins—and they are many—have been forgiven, so she has shown me much love. But a person who is forgiven little shows only little love" (Luke 7:47).

In that moment, everything made sense. Her story. Her tears. Her perfume. Her boldness. Her brokenness.

She loved much because she had been forgiven much.

That jar was the most valuable thing she owned. But it wasn't the perfume that was poured out that day—it was her. Her whole heart. Her whole life. And Jesus received it like the most sacred offering.

It changed me.

Jesus wasn't just forgiving a prostitute that day. He was offering sight to a blind Pharisee. He was offering grace to the judged and the judgers. Because we all need Him. We all have jars. And we all have the choice: hold onto them, or break them open and give it all.

Later, I asked God, What's my alabaster jar?

I expected a list. A specific answer.

But what I sensed was this: "It's your life."

Not your money. Not your talents. Not your schedule. Your whole life.

It sounds simple, but it's not. It's everything.

God created it all. He owns it all. And yet, He gave everything to us. His Son. His Spirit. His Kingdom. We are not just forgiven—we are called. We are heirs. And we are invited to give it all back.

What's your jar?

What are you holding onto that you haven't yet broken open?

Let it break.

Pour it out.

He's worth every drop.

Scriptures: Luke 7:36-50

Sending Out

THE MORNING AIR WAS soft as we stood gathered around Him. The Sea of Galilee shimmered behind us, and the sound of water lapping the shore seemed almost holy in its rhythm. There were twelve of us—so different in background, yet knit together by His call. Fishermen, a tax collector, a zealot... men who would never have chosen each other, but He had chosen us.

Jesus' eyes met mine, and my heart skipped. His gaze always seemed to search deeper depths than I knew I had. Then He spoke words that changed everything! He gave us His authority—to heal the sick, to cast out demons, to even raise the dead. I could hardly take it in. My hands, scarred from years of pulling nets, would now carry heaven's touch.

He called us each by name, one after another. Simon Peter—me, the impulsive one, the one who too often speaks before he thinks. Yet even I was included. I felt both unworthy and humbled.

"Go to the lost sheep of Israel," He said, His voice full of compassion. "Announce to them that the Kingdom of Heaven is near. Heal, cleanse, cast out, give freely as you have freely received." (Matthew 10:6–8 NLT)

The Kingdom of Heaven is near. His words filled me with both awe and trembling. Near—not a distant promise, but here, breaking in through us. I wanted to shout it to the world, yet I also wondered—would my faith be strong enough?

He told us not to take money, not even a spare tunic or sandals. To go empty-handed but full of trust. My old fisherman's heart wrestled with that. I always thought about tomorrow's catch, about security. Yet He was teaching us that the Father would be our provision. That every step would be met with His care.

Then His words grew sober.

"I am sending you out as sheep among wolves. Be as wise as serpents and harmless as doves. You will be handed over to courts, flogged in synagogues. You will stand before rulers because of me. But when that happens, don't worry about what to say. The Spirit of your Father will speak through you." (Matthew 10:16–20 NLT)

The Spirit of the Father... in me. That thought steadied my racing heart. My words had failed so often, but His Spirit would not.

He warned us of betrayals—brothers, fathers, children turning against their own. Hatred because of His name. A knot formed deep within. It was frightening, yet then He gave the hope that anchored me: "The one who endures to the end will be saved." (Matthew 10:22 NLT)

His voice softened as He looked at us with such tenderness:

"Don't be afraid of those who can kill the body but cannot touch the soul. Look at the sparrows—two sold for a penny. Not one falls without your Father knowing. And the very hairs on your head are all numbered. So don't be afraid—you are more valuable to God than a whole flock of sparrows." (Matthew 10:28–31 NLT)

I felt tears sting my eyes. More valuable than sparrows... every hair counted. The Father's love reached closer than I'd ever imagined. To think—He saw me, not just as one in the crowd, but known, cherished, held.

Jesus said that to follow Him meant to love Him above even family, above even life itself. His words cut like a blade, yet they healed at the same time. To lose my life for His sake would mean to find it. I didn't fully understand it, but my heart longed to live it.

Then He ended with the gentlest promise: "Anyone who receives you receives me. And even a cup of cold water given to the least of my followers will not lose its reward."
(Matthew 10:40, 42 NLT)

A cup of water. Something so small, yet seen by the Father. His Kingdom was not just in great miracles but in every act of kindness, every whisper of faith.

As I stood there, my fears and hopes tangled together, I realized this: He believed in us. He believed in me. And because He did, I could step forward—trembling maybe, but trusting—into the mission of heaven.

Scriptures: Matthew 10:1-40

Nicodemus: The Pharasee

THAT NIGHT, THE STREETS of Jerusalem were quiet. The Passover crowds had settled, and the faint smell of smoke drifted from the lamps and fires that still burned in the courtyards. My robe brushed the stone as I walked, My heart was racing, each beat echoing through me. I was Nicodemus—a Pharisee, a ruler among my people—respected, educated, a teacher of the Law. Yet something in me trembled.

I had heard Him in the temple courts, this Jesus of Nazareth. His words cut deeper than any rabbi's, His miracles undeniable. No trick of man could do the things I saw with my own eyes—the lame walking, the sick healed, demons cast out with a single command. Some of my peers mocked Him. Others burned with jealousy. But I could not ignore the stirring inside me, the questions I could no longer silence.

I approached the place where He stayed, the faint glow of a lamp inside flickering against the wooden doorframe. My throat was dry. I rehearsed my words, though they stumbled in my mind. I wanted to sound steady, confident, but the truth was I felt like a child again, reaching for something I could not grasp.

When I entered, He was there—calm, steady, His eyes like fire and mercy all at once. I spoke first, my voice breaking the silence. "Rabbi, we all know that God has sent You to teach us. Your miraculous signs are evidence that God is with You."

Even as the words left my mouth, I felt the weight of them. I wanted to say more, to ask what I truly longed for—what must I do to find eternal life? How can I be sure? But before I could untangle my thoughts, He looked at me, straight through me, and answered what I had not yet spoken aloud.

"I tell you the truth, unless you are born again, you cannot see the Kingdom of God."

The words struck me like a hammer against stone. Born again? My mind raced. How could He say this? I blurted out the confusion that pressed against me. "What do you mean? How can an old man go back into his mother's womb and be born again?"

He leaned forward slightly, His voice steady, sure, filled with a depth I had never heard before. "I assure you, no one can enter the Kingdom of God without being born of water and the Spirit. Humans can reproduce only human life, but the Holy Spirit gives birth to spiritual life. So don't be surprised when I say, 'You must be born again.' The wind blows wherever it wants. Just as you can hear the wind but can't tell where it comes from or where it is going, so you can't explain how people are born of the Spirit."

The air in the room seemed to shift as He spoke. I could almost feel the breeze He described, invisible yet undeniable. Still,

I whispered, almost ashamed of my own blindness, "How are these things possible?"

He looked at me—not with scorn, but with an ache, as though my ignorance grieved Him. "You are a respected Jewish teacher, and yet you don't understand these things? I assure you, we tell you what we know and have seen, and yet you won't believe our testimony. But if you don't believe me when I tell you about earthly things, how can you possibly believe if I tell you about heavenly things? No one has ever gone to heaven and returned. But the Son of Man has come down from heaven."

The way He spoke—it was as if He stood between heaven and earth, as if He Himself was the bridge. He went on, His voice quiet, yet it filled every corner of me.

"And as Moses lifted up the bronze snake on a pole in the wilderness, so the Son of Man must be lifted up, so that everyone who believes in Him will have eternal life. For this is how God loved the world: He gave His one and only Son, so that everyone who believes in Him will not perish but have eternal life. God sent His Son into the world not to judge the world, but to save the world through Him."

My eyes stung with tears I did not expect. Love. Not judgment. Salvation, not condemnation.

But He did not stop there. His words dug deep, unmasking the heart of every man. "There is no judgment against anyone who believes in Him. But anyone who does not believe in Him has already been judged for not believing in God's one and only Son.

And the judgment is based on this fact: God's light came into the world, but people loved the darkness more than the light, for their actions were evil. All who do evil hate the light and refuse to go near it, for fear their sins will be exposed. But those who do what is right come to the light so others can see that they are doing what God wants."

His gaze held mine, and I could not turn away. His words pierced me, not with condemnation, but with truth—truth that left me stripped of all my titles, my robes, my learning. I thought of my own life, the hidden pride, the fear of what my fellow Pharisees would say if they knew I was here. I thought of the darkness I had cloaked myself in, even while teaching others the Law.

And yet, for the first time, I wanted the Light more than I feared exposure.

I left that night with my steps unsteady, the cool night air brushing my face, carrying with it the weight of His words. I had come with questions, trying to appear wise, but He had answered with truth that shook me to the core.

I did not yet understand it all, but I knew this: the Kingdom of God was not something to be studied from afar—it was standing right in front of me. And slowly, against the fears and doubts of my Pharisee's heart, I began to believe.

Scriptures: John 3:1-21

The Well

THE SUN WAS HIGH, the heat pressing down on my shoulders like a heavy blanket. I had timed my walk carefully, when no one else would be near the well. Morning and evening were for the others—those who laughed and whispered together as they drew water. I avoided them. Their eyes, their words, their judgment. Better to bear the weight of the jar alone under the midday sun than endure their scorn.

As I approached, the stone mouth of Jacob's well shimmered in the light. Someone was sitting there. A man. A Jew. My stomach tightened. Jews despised us Samaritans. They would rather walk around our land than set foot in it. I pulled my veil closer, hoping maybe I could just draw quickly and leave unnoticed.

But He looked up. His eyes were steady, not harsh like others I had known. Then He spoke words I never expected: "Please give me a drink."

I froze. The accent betrayed Him—definitely a Jew. My thoughts tumbled. Why would He, a Jewish man, ask me, a Samaritan woman, for water? So I asked Him outright, my voice tinged with suspicion: "You are a Jew, and I am a Samaritan woman. Why are you asking me for a drink?"

He didn't answer with insult or rebuke. Instead, His words startled me: "If you only knew the gift God has for you and who you are speaking to, you would ask Me, and I would give you living water."

I blinked, confused. Living water? I glanced at the well, then at His empty hands. "But Sir, You don't have a rope or a bucket," I said, trying to reason it out. "This well is very deep. Where would You get this living water? And besides, do You think You're greater than our ancestor Jacob, who gave us this well? How can You offer better water than he and his sons and animals enjoyed?"

His gaze held mine, calm yet burning with a depth I couldn't explain. "Anyone who drinks this water will soon become thirsty again. But those who drink the water I give will never be thirsty again. It becomes a fresh, bubbling spring within them, giving them eternal life."

The words struck something in me. My heart ached with longing. Never thirst again? Never return to this place of shame, carrying this heavy jar day after day? I almost laughed with desperation. "Please, Sir," I pleaded, "give me this water! Then I'll never be thirsty again, and I won't have to come here to get water."

But then His words pierced deeper, beyond the surface. "Go and get your husband."

I stiffened. My spirit shrank within me as shame rose like a tide. "I don't have a husband," I answered quickly.

His reply shattered me: "You're right! You don't have a hus-band—for you have had five husbands, and you aren't even married to the man you're living with now. You certainly spoke the truth!"

How could He know? He named my hidden story without ever meeting me. My soul felt exposed. I tried to change the subject, retreating to religion, to what I knew. "Sir, You must be a prophet. So tell me—why is it that You Jews insist Jerusalem is the only place of worship, while we Samaritans claim it is here at Mount Gerizim, where our ancestors worshiped?"

He didn't argue. Instead, His words unfolded like light: "Believe Me, dear woman, the time is coming when it will no longer matter whether you worship the Father on this mountain or in Jerusalem. You Samaritans know very little about the one you worship, while we Jews know all about Him, for salvation comes through the Jews. But the time is coming—indeed it's here now—when true worshipers will worship the Father in Spirit and in truth. The Father is looking for those who will worship Him that way. For God is Spirit, so those who worship Him must worship in Spirit and in truth."

My lips trembled. I had heard whispers, stories of the One who would come. "I know the Messiah is coming—the One who is called Christ. When He comes, He will explain everything to us."

For years that promise had been like a dim lantern in the back of my soul—something my ancestors had clung to, though I won-dered if it could ever really be true for someone like me. Could the

Messiah possibly care about a Samaritan woman? Could He know my tangled life and still draw near?

Then He said the words that split through the shadows: "I Am the Messiah!"

The sound of His voice seemed to echo beyond the well, beyond the dusty hills, into the very marrow of my bones. My throat tightened, tears pricked my eyes. I couldn't move, couldn't speak, only stand there trembling as the reality settled on me. The One we had been waiting for—He was not in Jerusalem, not on Mount Gerizim, not hidden in some distant story. He was here, sitting across from me, speaking directly into my brokenness.

Just then, His followers came back, carrying food from the village. They looked shocked to find Him speaking with me, though none dared question Him aloud. I could feel their stares, but they no longer held me in chains. Shame lost its grip in the light of His words.

I left my water jar there by the well. The very reason I had come no longer mattered. My legs carried me back to the village faster than I thought possible, my heart pounding with something new—hope.

I called out to the people, my voice urgent and alive: "Come and see a man who told me everything I ever did! Could He possibly be the Messiah?"

The same villagers I once avoided turned their faces toward me. Curiosity flickered in their eyes. They saw my excitement, the wonder trembling in my voice, and one by one, they began to follow me.

Back at the well, the crowd gathered. They listened, they questioned, and soon they begged Him to stay. And He did—two whole days among us. He spoke words that quenched thirst we didn't even know we carried.

By the time He left, our village was changed. Many said to me, "Now we believe, not just because of what you told us, but because we have heard Him ourselves. Now we know that He is indeed the Savior of the world."

And I—once hidden in shame, avoiding the crowd at noon—had become the one to bring them to Him. I had gone to the well weary and thirsty. I left with living water, overflowing into the lives of others.

Scripture: John 4:1–42

12 Years

WHEN WE LANDED ON the western shore, the crowd was already waiting. The noise rose like a wave—shouts, cries, the sound of sandals scraping over stones, children darting forward, elders leaning on their staffs. The smell of sweat and fish hung heavy in the sun. People pressed closer, their faces alight with hope, their bodies crowding us so tightly I could hardly move.

Then Jairus came. A ruler of the synagogue, known by all, a man whose voice usually carried authority. But today his voice carried only desperation. His fine robes dragged in the dust as he fell at Jesus' feet. His cry cut the air: "My little daughter is dying. Please come and lay your hands on her; heal her so she can live."

I had never seen him like this—broken, overcome, humbled before the Teacher. His reputation could not save her. His learning, his position, his wealth—none of it mattered against death's shadow. All that remained was a father's love.

Jesus did not hesitate. He turned and went with him, and we followed. But the crowd surged around us, a pressing wall of bodies, the heat of humanity choking the narrow street.

And then—unseen at first—she came. A woman bent low, her eyes darting, her hands trembling. For twelve long years she had bled. Twelve years of weakness, of doctors and failed remedies, of spending everything she had until nothing remained. But worse than the sickness was the shame. Our law marked her unclean. Anyone she touched was defiled. Family would shrink away. Friends vanished. Strangers cursed her for daring to be near. Anger, fear, rejection—those were her companions. No one wanted her. No one cared.

Yet in her heart, a flicker of faith remained. She believed one thing: If I can just touch His robe, I will be healed.

Through the crush of people she reached. Her fingers brushed the fabric. And in an instant, strength flowed into her body, warmth surged through her, and she knew—her suffering was over. But it wasn't only her body that changed. Shame was broken. Rejection lifted. For the first time in twelve years, she belonged.

Jesus stopped. "Who touched My robe?" His voice cut through the chaos. We looked at Him, confused. Peter muttered, "Look at this crowd pressing around You. How can You ask who touched You?" But Jesus waited. He knew.

Trembling, she came forward and fell at His feet—the same place Jairus had fallen moments earlier. Her confession spilled out, raw and unhidden. The years of misery. The touch. The healing. The silence thickened. She braced for rebuke.

Instead, His words washed over her like life itself: "Daughter, your faith has made you well. Go in peace. Your suffering is over."

Daughter. Not outcast. Not unclean. Not forgotten. For twelve years she had been unwanted, and in one moment Jesus gave her a name of belonging.

Yet even as her heart soared, Jairus' heart broke. Messengers arrived with the words no parent ever wants to hear: "Your daughter is dead. There's no use troubling the Teacher now."

I watched his shoulders sag, the color drain from his face. He had clung to hope, but now despair crushed him. His daughter, only twelve years old—the same number of years this woman had suffered—was gone. One had lived twelve years in torment; the other had lived twelve years in innocence. Both were beyond human help.

But Jesus looked straight into Jairus' grief and said, "Don't be afraid. Just believe."

When we reached his home, the sound of mourning filled the air—shrill cries, wails of women, the tearing of garments, the bitter stench of grief. Inside, sorrow clung to the walls. But Jesus silenced them: "Why all this commotion and weeping? The child isn't dead; she's only asleep." They laughed at Him, mocking the hope He carried.

He sent them out and brought only Peter, James, me—John, and the parents into the room. The girl lay still, pale and lifeless, her small frame fragile in the lamplight.

Jesus knelt beside her, took her cold hand, and whispered, "Talitha koum—Little girl, get up."

Her eyes opened. Color rushed into her cheeks. She sat up, then stood and walked. Life had returned where death reigned. Her parents gasped, their cries turning from sorrow to joy too deep for words. Jesus, ever practical, told them to give her something to eat.

Two daughters. One bound in suffering for twelve years, now healed and restored. One bound by death at twelve years old, now raised to life. Both helpless, both hopeless—until Love Himself touched them.

And I saw the Kingdom that day. A Kingdom that sees the desperate father and the outcast woman. A Kingdom where twelve years of shame and twelve years of joy both matter to God. A Kingdom where death yields to His voice, and rejection dissolves in His love. A Kingdom not distant, but here, moving among us through Jesus.

Scriptures: Mark 5:21-43

The 72

WE WERE STANDING AMONG the others when the Lord's eyes swept across us with such deep compassion. That day He appointed seventy-two of us to be sent out, two by two. A wave of reverence swept through me when His hand landed on Philip, then mine. Out of the many who followed Him, we were set apart for this mission.

Philip leaned close, his voice barely above a whisper. "Stephen, we've been appointed among the seventy-two... entrusted with His work."

I could only nod, a weight pressing within me—sent by Jesus to carry His message to towns and villages He Himself would soon visit. He spoke of a harvest so vast, fields upon fields waiting to be gathered in, yet so few workers. Then came His charge: "Now go."

He warned us—no money bag, no extra sandals, no lingering along the way. Go dependent. Go vulnerable. Go like lambs among wolves. Yet His words carried a strength that steadied my trembling.

We set out, the road stretching before us in heat and dust. Our voices trembled the first time we entered a home and declared, "Peace to this house." Something unseen settled there. The family welcomed us with joy. Bread still warm from the fire, figs pulled from the tree, a clay cup of cool water—each meal felt like a feast provided by the hand of God.

But not every village welcomed us. Once, we entered a town with hopeful hearts, speaking peace at the gate. Faces turned hard, arms folded, words muttered with scorn. Doors shut. The market grew silent at our approach. Philip and I glanced at each other, heavy-hearted. Then, with trembling hands, we followed Jesus' instructions—wiping the dust of that town from our feet as a sign. "Know this," Philip said aloud, his voice steady though his eyes burned, "the Kingdom of God has come near to you."

Later that night, by the fire, he whispered, "Stephen, it hurts to be rejected. Yet His words come back to me—'the one who rejects you rejects Me.'" We sat long in the silence, tears glistening in the firelight.

But there were other moments—moments that set our hearts aflame. One day, as we entered a small village, a man hobbled toward us on a twisted leg, pain etched across his face. His family begged us to pray. Philip laid his hand upon him, and together we spoke the name of Jesus. I watched in awe as the man straightened, his leg strengthened before our eyes. He laughed—oh, what a laugh!—and began to walk without pain. The whole village came running, and we proclaimed to them, "The Kingdom of God is near you today."

Another time, we encountered a boy tormented by an evil spirit. His parents wept as he thrashed on the ground, foam at his mouth. Fear gripped me, but I remembered the Lord's words. Kneeling, I cried out, "In the name of Jesus Christ, come out of him!" At once, the boy went still. His eyes cleared. He sat up, whispering, "I'm free." His mother clung to him, sobbing into his hair. Philip's shoulders shook as he wept beside them.

Again and again, power flowed—not from us, but through us, from Him. At night, lying beneath the stars, our whispers were filled with awe.

"Why would He entrust us with this?" Philip asked one evening, staring into the heavens.

"Because this is who He is," I said, though my own heart quivered at the thought. "He calls the weak and shows His power through them. It is never about us."

When at last we returned, the courtyard pulsed with life. Every pair had stories—laughter, tears, wonders. The air buzzed with joy. Philip and I stepped forward, our voices unsteady with awe. "Lord," we cried, "even the demons obey us when we use Your name!"

Jesus' smile broke across His face, filled with both joy and solemn weight. "Yes," He said, "I saw Satan fall from heaven like lightning! Look, I have given you authority over all the power of the enemy. Nothing will injure you."

But then His voice grew tender, and His words pierced deeper than all we had seen: "But don't rejoice because evil spirits obey you; rejoice because your names are registered in heaven."

I had been rejoicing in the wonders, the healings, the freedom—but He was saying that the truest miracle was that we belonged to God. My name—Stephen—written in His eternal book. Philip's name, too. Not forgotten. Not overlooked. Known by the Father Himself.

As this sank in, Jesus lifted His eyes toward heaven, His face radiant. He was full of joy—joy unlike any I had ever seen. His voice trembled with love as He prayed, "O Father, Lord of heaven and earth, thank you for hiding these things from those who think themselves wise and clever, and for revealing them to the childlike. Yes, Father, it pleased you to do it this way."

Tears stung my eyes. To see Jesus rejoice—truly rejoice in the Father—was more powerful than all the miracles we had witnessed. It was as though heaven itself had broken open before us.

Philip leaned close, his voice hushed and thick with emotion. "Stephen, this—this is the greatest gift. Not power, not authority, but that He knows us, and we know Him."

And I knew, whatever lay ahead, I would never be the same.

Scriptures: Luke 10:1-24

Religious Law Expert

THE SUN HAD ALREADY risen high when I left my home that morning, the scroll of Deuteronomy still fresh in my mind. I had been pouring over the words of Moses—commands we were given to live by, the way to righteousness, the path of obedience that set us apart as God's people. The Scriptures had always been my life. I was a rabbi, a teacher of the Law, a guide for the community. Yet, if I am honest, my heart was restless.

For weeks, whispers of this man, Jesus of Nazareth, had filled the courtyards of the Temple. Some said He was a prophet. Others, a troublemaker leading people away from the Law. A few dared to call Him Messiah. I longed to meet Him—not just out of curiosity, but because I felt something stirring deep inside me. Could He be the One? Or would I expose Him as a fraud who dishonored our traditions?

That morning, as I stepped into the marketplace, the air thick with dust and voices, I learned Jesus was nearby teaching a crowd. My pulse quickened. This was my moment. I would test Him, as any rabbi would. After all, if He was from God, His words would stand. If not, His folly would be clear.

I pushed through the crowd until I could see Him. He wasn't like the other teachers. No robes of honor. No air of superiority. He spoke with an authority that was not rehearsed, not borrowed. It unsettled me. My throat tightened, but I called out anyway, my voice carrying above the people:

"Teacher, what should I do to inherit eternal life?"

It was the question we all asked, wasn't it? What pleases God? How do we secure the life He promises? But if I am honest, I also wanted to test Him, to see if His answers would align with the Law I had devoted my life to.

He didn't answer directly. Instead, His eyes met mine—steady, piercing. Then He turned my question back on me. "What does the Law of Moses say? How do you read it?"

My lips moved almost without thought, words I had recited since childhood: "You must love the Lord your God with all your heart, all your soul, all your strength, and all your mind. And, love your neighbor as yourself."

"You are right," He said gently, but with weight. "Do this and you will live."

For a moment, I felt the ground give way beneath me. He had affirmed the Law, yes, but His words cut deeper. Do this. Live this. I knew the Law inside and out, but could I say I truly lived it? I felt the eyes of the crowd on me. My pride fought back. I couldn't be exposed as one lacking. So I asked again, searching for a way to justify myself, "And who is my neighbor?"

That's when He told the story.

A man was traveling from Jerusalem to Jericho, beaten and left for dead. A priest saw him and passed by. Then a Levite did the same. But a Samaritan—a Samaritan!—stopped, tended to the man's wounds, and cared for him at his own expense.

Every word landed like a hammer inside me. We despised Samaritans, called them unclean, less than us. Yet in His story, it was the Samaritan who embodied the very command I had quoted—the one who truly loved his neighbor.

"Now which of these three," Jesus asked, His gaze never leaving mine, "would you say was a neighbor to the man who was attacked?"

The answer burned on my tongue. I couldn't bring myself to say the word "Samaritan." So I muttered, "The one who showed him mercy."

"Now go," Jesus said, "and do the same."

His words haunted me long after the crowd dispersed. I had come to trap Him, but He had unwrapped my heart instead. I realized I had spent my life dissecting the Law, teaching it, guarding it—yet somewhere along the way, I had lost its very heartbeat. Loving God. Loving others. Mercy. Compassion. These were more than words to be studied; they were life to be lived.

That day, I met Jesus, and nothing was the same.

Scriptures: Luke 10:25-37

5000

THE SUN HAD JUST begun to rise over the hills when my mother handed me the basket. Inside were five small barley loaves she had baked that morning and two dried fish my father had caught the day before. "Keep this close," she told me with a smile, "it will be our food later."

I was young, the youngest among my brothers and sisters, but I held that basket with pride. Today was no ordinary day. For weeks, my family had spoken of a man named Jesus. Some of my uncles had heard Him speak before—words unlike any rabbi they had ever listened to. Others in our family had seen with their own eyes miracles that could not be explained. They told us of sick people healed, of demons driven out, and of a hope that stirred deep inside them. My parents wanted us all to come this time—to see Him for ourselves.

The roads were crowded as we walked, people streaming from villages and towns. Some leaned on staffs, others carried their children on their shoulders. All of them seemed to carry the same anticipation I felt. What would this man say? What would He do? Could He truly be the One we had waited for?

By midday we had followed the crowds to a grassy hillside overlooking the Sea of Galilee. The breeze carried the scent of water and wild grass. Families were spreading out, sitting on the ground, waiting for Him. And then, there He was. Jesus. He climbed a little higher up the slope, His disciples gathered near Him. When He began to speak, His voice carried across the hillside, strong yet full of compassion.

I couldn't take my eyes off Him. He spoke of the Kingdom of God as if He knew it better than anyone. It was as if Heaven itself poured from His lips. My parents nodded, my uncles leaned forward, and tears welled in my mother's eyes. I didn't understand everything, but I knew His words were alive.

The hours passed, and the sun began to dip low. I could hear stomachs growling all around us—my own included. We hadn't eaten, and we were far from home. Whispers rippled through the crowd. Some said we should leave to find food. Others didn't want to go—they didn't want to miss a single moment with Him.

Then I saw movement among His disciples. They were talking to Him, pointing at the thousands of people scattered on the grass. Jesus looked out over us all, then back at them. Something was happening.

Before I could think, one of the disciples—Andrew—noticed me clutching the basket. He crouched down, his eyes kind. "What do you have there, young one?"

I lifted the lid. "Just five loaves and two fish. My mother packed them."

He smiled gently, almost sadly. "It's not much for so many." Then he took me by the hand and led me to Jesus. The world fell away, leaving only the pounding rhythm of life and wonder in my veins.

Standing before Him, I could hardly breathe. Jesus looked at me—not just at my face, but deep into me, as if He could see my whole life, my whole heart. Yet His gaze was not heavy—it was full of love. Andrew spoke, "There's a boy here with five barley loaves and two fish, but what good is that with this huge crowd?"

Jesus reached toward me, His hands gentle. Without a word, I placed the basket in them. It seemed so small, laughable even, compared to the thousands sitting on the grass. But when His fingers wrapped around the basket, it no longer felt small.

He lifted His eyes toward Heaven and gave thanks. Then, breaking the loaves, He handed them to the disciples. They began to pass them out. First to those nearest Him, then farther and farther. My eyes grew wide as the food never ran out. The loaves kept breaking, the fish kept multiplying. What I had placed in His hands was becoming more than enough.

I sat on the grass, knees pulled up, clutching my tunic with trembling hands. My thoughts raced. How is this happening? Yet something inside me—the same childlike wonder I felt during the great feasts each year—whispered that it was God. I remembered the times when our family celebrated Passover, eating the lamb just as our ancestors had done in Egypt, telling again the story of God's mighty hand that delivered us. I remembered the Feast of

Tabernacles, when we made little shelters and rejoiced in how God provided in the wilderness. I remembered the stories of manna falling from Heaven, enough for each day.

As I watched bread multiply before my eyes, I thought, This is just like that! The same God who gave manna is here with us now. And Jesus... He must be the One God promised.

The crowd buzzed with laughter and joy. Children clapped their hands. Fathers and mothers looked at one another in wonder as they ate until they were full. Not just a taste, not just a bite—everyone had all they wanted.

When the baskets came back, overflowing with leftovers, I sat stunned. My small lunch had fed thousands. No—not my lunch. His blessing. His power. His love.

My heart swelled. As a child, I had always believed God could do anything. And here He was, showing me that nothing placed in His hands was ever too small.

That night as we walked home under the fading light of the stars, my mother placed her hand gently on my shoulder. Her touch was warm, steady, almost trembling with the weight of all she had seen. She leaned close and whispered, her voice thick with emotion, "Do you see, my son? This is why we came. To see with our own eyes the hand of God among us."

Her words sank deep into me. I clutched the empty basket tightly in my arms, still remembering how full it had once been, how bread and fish kept appearing as though Heaven itself had poured into it. I thought of the feasts we celebrated every year—how we told the stories of God's faithfulness long ago. But now, it wasn't just a story. I had seen it. I had tasted it.

I lifted my eyes to the sky, the same sky under which Abraham once counted stars, and I whispered in my heart, Yes, I see. In that moment, I knew—God was here, and Jesus was the One He had sent.

And with the simple trust of a child, I believed. That day would never leave me. It was written on my heart forever.

Scriptures: Matthew 14:13–21, Mark 6:30–44, Luke 9:12–17, and John 6:1–14

The Storm

THE STORM PRESSED DOWN on us that night with a fury that seemed almost alive. The wind shrieked as it tore across the lake, whipping the sail until we pulled it down, leaving us only the oars. My hands stung, torn raw from rope and wood, my shoulders burned from the endless straining. Salt spray lashed my face, stinging my eyes, leaving the taste of bitterness on my lips. Each wave lifted us high, then dropped us with a shudder that rattled the very frame of the boat.

The others groaned with the strain. John shouted above the roar, trying to keep rhythm with the oars. James gritted his teeth, his arms trembling from the weight of it all. Andrew's face was set like stone, sweat and spray streaming down his brow. Though we were fishermen, this storm mocked us, making us feel like children in a game we could not win. Fear clawed at each of us. I remember the way Thomas muttered prayers under his breath, and how Nathaniel gripped the side of the boat so tightly his knuckles were white.

Then—through the gloom, something moved across the surface of the water. At first it was only a shape, blurred by the rain, but it drew closer, sure and steady. My pulse thundered so loudly I could feel it everywhere. The others saw it too, and terror broke loose among us. Someone cried, "It's a ghost!" and the words ripped through the boat like fire. We shouted over one another, fear choking us more than the storm itself.

And then His voice. His voice—clear, calm, steady, as though no storm could touch Him. "Don't be afraid. Take courage. I am here!"

The sound of Him cut through my fear like light through darkness. My heart leapt—I knew it was the Lord. Everything in me longed to be near Him. So I shouted, my voice cracking in the wind, "Lord, if it's really You, tell me to come to You, walking on the water!"

He looked at me. Even through the storm, His gaze was steady. His answer was simple, but it carried the weight of heaven itself: "Come."

I swung my legs over the side, the boat slick beneath my hands, and my feet touched the water. It held me. I stood. The surface rippled, but it did not break beneath me. Filled with wonder, I took one step after another toward Him. The storm still raged—the spray struck my face, the wind whipped at my cloak—but as long as I fixed my eyes on Him, I stood.

But then my gaze shifted. The waves rose higher, the wind howled louder, and the storm pressed in on every side. Fear surged, and with it, the water opened beneath me. I plunged down into the icy depths. The cold swallowed my legs, pulling me under, and terror flooded my soul. "Lord! Save me!" I cried with all that was in me.

Immediately His hand was there. Strong. Firm. Unshakable. He caught me, lifting me out of the deep. His voice was gentle, but it pierced me: "Peter, you have so little faith. Why did you doubt Me?"

Together we climbed into the boat. The instant His foot touched the wood, the storm ceased. The winds hushed. The waves smoothed into stillness. A holy silence spread across the lake, heavy and thick, like the air itself bowed to Him.

We were shaken. James fell to his knees, his lips trembling. John whispered, barely able to breathe, "Truly... He is the Son of God." Andrew's face was pale, his eyes wide with awe. One of the others turned to me, his voice breaking, "Peter... you walked on the water."

I sat trembling, my body still dripping, my hand tingling from where He had gripped me. My eyes filled with tears as I whispered back, "Only because He was there. when I looked at the storm, I sank."

The hush of that night has never left me. The memory of His hand catching mine burns deeper than the storm, deeper than the waves. For I learned in that moment—when my eyes are fixed on Him, nothing can pull me under.

Scriptures: Matthew 14:22–33, Mark 6:45–52, John 6:16–21

Bread from Heaven

THE NEXT DAY, AS the crowd pressed around us on the far side of the lake, I could feel the weight of expectation in the air. They had seen Him feed thousands with just a few loaves and fish, and now they followed with hungry eyes, hoping for more.

I watched as Jesus turned to them, His voice steady and filled with authority: "I tell you the truth, you want to be with me because I fed you, not because you understood the miraculous signs. But don't be so concerned about perishable things like food. Spend your energy seeking the eternal life that the Son of Man can give you." (John 6:26–27 NLT)

My stomach tightened as He spoke. I knew these people—they wanted bread, not Him. They wanted their bellies filled, not their souls. Yet He was offering Himself, the very life of God in flesh.

The crowd pressed with questions, murmuring about Moses and the manna in the wilderness. Jesus answered with words that made the air feel heavier around us: "The true bread of God is the one who comes down from heaven and gives life to the world." (John 6:33 NLT)

I felt the sharp intake of breath from those gathered. They cried, "Sir, give us that bread every day!"

And then He said it—words so piercing I can still hear them ringing in my mind: "I am the bread of life. Whoever comes to me will never be hungry again. Whoever believes in me will never be thirsty." (John 6:35 NLT)

My whole being shuddered as He spoke. It was no longer about loaves and fish, but about Him—His life sustaining us forever. Yet, I could see the confusion and resistance on their faces. Whispers rippled through the crowd: Isn't this Jesus, the son of Joseph? How can he say, 'I came down from heaven'?

But He pressed on, undeterred by their grumbling. His words cut to the core: "I tell you the truth, anyone who believes has eternal life. Yes, I am the bread of life! Your ancestors ate manna in the wilderness, but they all died. Anyone who eats the bread from heaven, however, will never die." (John 6:47–50 NLT)

The moment hung thick with tension. And then He went deeper—words that caused even my own pulse to quicken: "Anyone who eats my flesh and drinks my blood remains in me, and I in him." (John 6:56 NLT)

A gasp spread through the synagogue. The words were too much for many. I felt the heat of anger rising from those around us. People shook their heads, offended, muttering that His teaching was intolerable. One by one, many who had followed Him turned away. I watched them leave, their sandals scuffing against the stone floor as they abandoned the very One who had come to give them life.

My heart ached. I didn't fully understand all His words either. They were mysterious, even unsettling. Yet in the depth of my being, I knew—I couldn't walk away. There was something about Him, about His voice, about the way life seemed to breathe through His words that anchored me even when I didn't grasp it all.

Jesus turned to us, the Twelve, His eyes searching ours. "Are you also going to leave?" (John 6:67 NLT)

The question pierced me. My lips trembled as the truth burned through my soul, and I spoke words that spilled from the deepest part of me: "Lord, to whom would we go? You have the words that give eternal life. We believe, and we know you are the Holy One of God." (John 6:68–69 NLT)

And now, I remember the silence after I spoke. The others looked at me—some with tears in their eyes, others slowly nodding in agreement. One of them whispered, "Peter, you spoke what was in all our hearts." Jesus then fixed His eyes on me, and in that gaze I knew He saw everything: my weakness, my questions, and my faith all at once.

I did not understand all He said that day. But I knew this: He was life itself, the bread from heaven. And no matter how many left, I could not. For where else would I go?

Scriptures: John 6:22-71

Feast of Tabernacles

THE FEAST OF TABERNACLES always brought life to Jerusalem. The streets were alive with pilgrims—songs rising into the air, families carrying palm branches, the smell of sacrifices mingling with bread baking in ovens. Yet underneath the celebration, the city was restless. The name on everyone's lips was Jesus of Nazareth.

Among my fellow Pharisees, anger simmered. Many were determined to silence him, to expose him as a fraud. They plotted in whispers and in open speech: "If he dares to appear, we must arrest him." I listened to them, but deep within, my thoughts turned elsewhere.

I could not shake the memory of my secret meeting with him one night, not long ago. The way his eyes had held mine as he told me truths that upended my understanding. "You must be born again." I had pressed him, confused, but he spoke with authority that cut deeper than any rabbinic debate I had ever known. He spoke of the Spirit, of a new birth, of God's love that would send His Son into the world—not to condemn, but to save. I had left that night unsettled, my mind racing, yet strangely alive. Something had stirred in me, something I could not deny.

Now, here he was in the Temple, teaching with boldness. He declared, "My message is not my own; it comes from God who sent me. Anyone who wants to do the will of God will know whether my teaching is from God or merely my own."

The Law, the Prophets, the Psalms—I had studied them since boyhood. And as he spoke, words I had memorized from Isaiah and Jeremiah, even the promise of Moses about a Prophet to come, began to burn in my mind. Could it be? Was he the fulfillment of all these things? My heart beat faster, torn between fear of my peers and the growing flame of faith within me.

Then came the moment I will never forget. On the last and greatest day of the Feast, when the priests poured water at the altar in remembrance of God's provision in the wilderness, Jesus cried out in the Temple courts, his voice like thunder echoing against the stone:

"Anyone who is thirsty may come to me! Anyone who believes in me may come and drink! For the Scriptures declare, 'Rivers of living water will flow from his heart.'"

The people froze, caught between awe and outrage. My whole being tensed. The water ceremony had always pointed to God's provision, and now this man claimed to be its fulfillment. In my mind, his midnight words returned: "Unless you are born of water and the Spirit, you cannot enter the Kingdom of God." Could this living water be what he meant?

The crowd was divided. Some cried, "He is the Prophet!" Others declared, "He is the Messiah!" Still others mocked, "The

Messiah cannot come from Galilee." Yet within me, the divisions of my own heart were slowly being healed. The more I heard him, the more the prophecies and teachings I had known since childhood began to converge. He was not contradicting the Law—he was embodying it. He was not breaking the promises—he was fulfilling them.

When the temple guards returned without arresting him, my peers were enraged. "Why didn't you bring him in?" they demanded. The guards' reply sent a shiver through me: "We have never heard anyone speak like this man!"

The chamber filled with ridicule. "Are you deceived too Nicodemus? None of us rulers believe in him. This crowd is accursed!"

Something in me snapped. I could not stay silent. I rose and asked, "Is it legal to convict a man before he is given a hearing?"

They turned on me at once. "Are you from Galilee, too? Search the Scriptures and see for yourself—no prophet ever comes from Galilee!"

Their words stung, but even more, they revealed the blindness of our hearts. We were so consumed with disproving him that we refused to see what stood before us. I sank into silence, but inside, faith grew. I remembered the night under the stars, when he had spoken to me of God's love. I remembered his words today, rivers of living water. Piece by piece, the veil was lifting.

My heart longed to seek him, to know him—not just as teacher, but as Messiah. I was not there yet, but I was closer. The law I had studied all my life was not leading me away from him—it was leading me to him. And I knew the day would come when silence would no longer be possible.

Scriptures: John 7:1-52

The Woman

THE MORNING AIR IN Jerusalem was still cool as I walked through the temple courts with the other men of the council. The city was waking, pilgrims moving about, priests preparing sacrifices, merchants arranging their stalls. But my mind was already fixed on a task. We had spoken of it the night before—this man Jesus. He had become too great a threat. His words stirred the crowds, his teaching was unlike anything we had heard, and worse still, he did not seek our approval. He did not bend to our traditions. Instead, he claimed authority as if from God Himself.

We, the guardians of the Law, could not allow him to continue unchecked. Too many people hung on his every word, whispering that perhaps he was the Messiah. But he could not be—he had no formal training under the great rabbis, and he challenged us in public. He disregarded the fences we had built around the Torah, the very traditions that kept Israel set apart. If the people turned after him, our influence, even our nation's order, could be shaken.

So, we plotted. What trap could be set that would force him to reveal himself for what we believed him to be—either a lawbreaker or a pretender? The Law of Moses was our ground, our strength.

And then word came to us—a woman, caught in the very act of adultery. The timing seemed perfect. The Law was clear: such a woman deserved death. If Jesus excused her, he would be defying Moses. If he condemned her, the Romans—who alone reserved the right of execution—could be told he was inciting rebellion. Either way, we would have him.

We seized her in the act, dragging her into the streets, her hair disheveled, her face streaked with shame and fear. I remember the eyes of the crowd as they turned toward us—some curious, others scandalized. Her disgrace was now a public spectacle, and we intended it so. The more public this became, the tighter the noose around Jesus would grow.

When we reached him, he was seated, teaching the people in the temple courts. They hung on His every word, as if His words were living bread. I burned with indignation. Who was he to command such attention? Who was he to speak as if he had authority over the holy Law?

I stepped forward, pushing the woman into the circle before him. My voice was loud enough for all to hear. "Teacher, this woman was caught in the act of adultery. The Law of Moses says to stone her. What do you say?"

Inside, I felt the thrill of the moment. The crowd was watching, every ear bent to hear his answer. He was cornered. We had set the perfect snare.

But he did not answer. Instead, he bent down and began writing in the dust with his finger. My face flushed. Was he ignoring us?

Was he mocking us? Around me, the others pressed the question again and again.

Finally, he straightened. His eyes, steady and piercing, looked through us, not just at us. "All right," he said, "but let the one who has never sinned throw the first stone."

His words landed like a hammer blow. My grip tightened around the stone in my hand. The Law was clear, yet suddenly, his words cut deeper than the Law. They cut into my own soul. The weight of my own failures pressed heavy upon me. I tried to fight it—remind myself of my years of training, my careful keeping of the statutes, my zeal for righteousness. But I could not shake the truth: I was not without sin. None of us were.

The silence was suffocating. One by one, beginning with the oldest among us, the stones dropped from our hands. The sound of each stone hitting the ground seemed to echo our defeat. We had come to trap him, and yet he exposed us instead.

I turned and walked away, shame burning my face, though I tried not to show it. We had failed again. This Jesus was not so easily cornered.

As I left, I could still hear his voice, gentle now, speaking to the woman: "Where are your accusers? Didn't even one of them condemn you?"

"No, Lord," she whispered.

"Neither do I. Go and sin no more."

His words rang in my ears long after. We had come to prove him against the Law of Moses, but instead, he revealed the heart of God—mercy, holiness, truth woven together. And though I resisted it, deep inside something stirred, something I dared not name: could it be that he was more than a man?

Scriptures: John 8:1-11

Blindness

THE ROAD OUTSIDE THE Temple was alive with voices that day, the hum of merchants, pilgrims, and the shuffle of sandaled feet. I had sat there for years, a fixture on the stone path. Most didn't even look at me anymore. To them, I was just another beggar. To me, I was trapped in an endless night.

I had been blind from the moment I was born. My mother told me often how she had prayed over me, weeping into the night as she held me close. My father worked hard, but our family carried the shame of my condition. People whispered that my blindness must be a curse, the punishment for some hidden sin—either mine, though I had not yet lived, or theirs. The weight of those words pressed down heavier than any cloak I ever wrapped around myself.

Every day, I learned to listen to the world differently than others did. The crackle of firewood told me where warmth was. The quick step of children darting past brought me a bittersweet pang—I would never chase or run as they did. The clink of coins in a passerby's hand gave me hope they might drop one into my bowl. But most often, I only heard silence—people avoiding me, stepping wide, not wanting to be reminded of my brokenness.

That morning, as I sat in my usual place, I heard voices pause near me. I could tell by the weight in their tone that they were speaking of me, not to me. They asked a Rabbi—a man called Jesus, whom I had begun to hear rumors about—"Why was this man born blind? Was it because of his own sins or his parents' sins?"

I braced myself for another round of debate over my worth. But His reply startled me. He said, "It was not because of his sins or his parents' sins. This happened so the power of God could be seen in him."

For the first time in my life, someone had spoken of my blindness not as a curse, but as a canvas for God's glory.

Then I heard Him kneel down close. There was the sound of spitting, then the grit of dirt being mixed. Before I could ask, I felt cool, damp clay pressed gently upon my eyes. His hands were firm yet kind. And then His voice, steady and commanding, told me, "Go, wash yourself in the pool of Siloam."

Stumbling to my feet, guided by memory of the streets and the staff in my hand, I made my way. Each step was filled with both fear and hope. When I knelt at the pool's edge and splashed the water onto my eyes, light—blinding, brilliant, overwhelming light—burst into my darkness. Shapes, colors, movement. For the first time, I saw water rippling. I saw my own trembling hands. Tears mixed with the pool as I laughed and cried at once.

I returned home, and people stared in disbelief. Some insisted I was not the same man, only someone who looked like me. But I kept saying, "Yes, I am the one! The man they call Jesus healed me!"

The leaders, however, were not pleased. They dragged me into questioning again and again. "This man healed you on the Sabbath," they accused. "He cannot be from God."

But how could I deny the truth? I told them plainly, "I was blind, and now I see." That one fact was more than all their arguments.

They questioned my parents, fearful people who simply said, "He is our son, and he was born blind. But how he can now see, ask him. He is old enough to speak for himself."

So they brought me back, trying to trap me with their words. I answered them with boldness I did not know I had: "Ever since the world began, no one has been able to open the eyes of someone born blind. If this man were not from God, He couldn't have done it."

Their rage boiled over, and they threw me out. But even as the Temple doors slammed behind me, I felt freer than ever before.

Later, He found me again. Jesus. The sound of His voice was already familiar, but this time, I saw His face. He asked me, "Do you believe in the Son of Man?"

"Who is He, sir?" I asked, "Tell me so I may believe."

"You have seen Him," Jesus said, "and He is speaking to you."

My knees gave way. "Yes, Lord, I believe!" I said, and I worshiped Him right there.

Some Pharisees stood nearby, their faces twisted with scorn. Jesus looked at them and said, "I entered this world to render judgment—to give sight to the blind and to show those who think they see that they are blind."

Their voices bristled with pride. "Are You saying we're blind?"

Jesus' words fell heavy as stone: "If you were blind, you wouldn't be guilty. But you remain guilty because you claim you can see."

I knew then He wasn't only speaking of physical eyes. My darkness had been lifted in a single act of mercy. Theirs remained, not because they could not see, but because they refused to. Spiritual blindness was far worse than the life I had known in darkness. I had lived blind, but humble. They lived in pride, blind to the truth standing before them.

That day I realized being cast out by them was nothing compared to being welcomed in by Him.

Scriptures: John 9:1–41

Lazarus

I REMEMBER THE FIRST time Jesus came into our home. I wanted everything to be perfect—bread baked, the lamb seasoned just right, oil and wine ready for our guest. I hurried about making sure every detail was in place, while Mary sat at His feet, drinking in every word. I grew frustrated with her, but Jesus gently reminded me that she had chosen what mattered most. His words stung at first, but they also stayed with me. From that day, He became more than a guest to us. He was our teacher, our friend, and our Lord.

So when Lazarus grew sick, I knew exactly what to do. We sent a message quickly: "Lord, your dear friend is very sick." At that time He was across the Jordan, nearly a day's journey from us. In my heart I thought surely He would come right away. He had healed so many—would He not come quickly to the one He loved?

Later, I learned how He responded when the news reached Him. Instead of hurrying, He stayed where He was for two more days. He told His disciples, "This sickness will not end in death. No, it happened for the glory of God, so that the Son of God will receive glory from this." And then He said to them, "Our friend Lazarus has fallen asleep, but now I will go and wake him up."

They did not understand. "Lord, if he is sleeping, he will soon get better." But Jesus spoke plainly, "Lazarus is dead. And for your sakes, I'm glad I wasn't there, for now you will really believe. Come, let's go to him."

How different His view was from ours. To us, death was an end. We wrapped the body, sealed it in the tomb, and wept because it felt so final. But to Him, the giver of life, death was only sleep—temporary, waiting for His call.

Meanwhile, Lazarus weakened before my eyes. I sat by his side, praying, listening as his breathing slowed. Then it stopped. My brother was gone. Our house filled with mourners. For four days I lived in sorrow, hearing wails, receiving condolences, but feeling only emptiness. Each sound of footsteps outside made me look up, hoping it was Jesus. But it never was.

At last word came that He was near. I could not stay in the house a moment longer. I ran to meet Him on the road. My words tumbled out with both grief and faith: "Lord, if only you had been here, my brother would not have died. But even now I know that God will give you whatever you ask."

He looked at me with calm certainty. "Your brother will rise again."

"Yes, Lord," I said. "He will rise when everyone else rises, at the last day." That was what I believed, what I had been taught. But He spoke again, and His words shook me to the core:

"I am the resurrection and the life. Anyone who believes in me will live, even after dying. Everyone who lives in me and believes in me will never ever die. Do you believe this, Martha?"

I had always believed in a coming resurrection, but now Resurrection Himself stood in front of me. Life was looking into my eyes. "Yes, Lord," I said, slowly but surely. "I have always believed you are the Messiah, the Son of God, the one who has come into the world from God."

I hurried back and whispered to Mary, "The Teacher is here and wants to see you." She rose quickly, and soon I watched as she fell at His feet, sobbing, "Lord, if only you had been here, my brother would not have died!" Her sorrow stirred Him deeply.

"Where have you laid him?" He asked.

We led Him to the tomb. And there, to my astonishment, He wept. The One who healed strangers and spoke of eternal life wept beside us. Some whispered, "See how much He loved him." Others grumbled, "Couldn't He have kept Lazarus from dying?"

Then Jesus commanded, "Roll the stone aside."

I hesitated. "Lord, he has been dead four days. The smell will be terrible."

"Didn't I tell you," He answered, "that you would see God's glory if you believe?"

The stone was moved. The air carried the sharp stench of death. Jesus lifted His eyes in prayer, then cried out with authority, "Lazarus, come out!"

For one suspended moment, everything was silent. Then—movement. The sound of footsteps. My brother came out of the tomb, still wrapped in strips of cloth, but alive.

"Unwrap him and let him go!" Jesus commanded.

I could not contain my tears or my joy. My brother was alive. Death, which to us had felt so permanent, had been only sleep to Him. With one word, He woke Lazarus up.

Many who stood there believed that day, their faces filled with wonder. Others hurried off to report it to the Pharisees. But for me, nothing could ever be the same again.

I once thought faith was believing Jesus could heal. Now I know—He is Lord over death itself. What we call final, He calls temporary. Where we see an ending, He speaks awakening. When He comes, life comes with Him.

Scriptures: John 11:1-57

Zaccheus

I WAS A MAN despised. Everyone in Jericho knew my name, though not with honor. I was the chief tax collector, rich by the coins I took from my own people to feed the empire of Rome. My wealth was abundant, but my soul was hollow. Though my home was filled with fine things, laughter never echoed there, and peace never rested under my roof. I was seen as a traitor, a sinner, unworthy of God's love.

Yet something stirred in me when I heard that Jesus was passing through our city. His name had spread across the land—He healed the sick, gave sight to the blind, and spoke of God's Kingdom with an authority unlike anything we had known. My heart longed for a glimpse of Him, though I could not explain why.

The streets that day were crowded. I am a small man, and I could not see above the throng pressing in to catch sight of Him. So, without shame, I ran ahead and climbed into a sycamore-fig tree along the road. My robes snagged on the bark, but I did not care—I had to see Him.

When Jesus came near, He stopped beneath the very branches where I perched. He lifted His eyes, and in that moment it was as if

He saw into the depths of who I was. He spoke my name—not "tax collector," not "traitor," but my name, Zacchaeus. "Quick, come down! I must be a guest in your home today."

I nearly fell from the tree, so overcome was I with shock and joy. No teacher, no rabbi, no righteous man had ever desired to sit under my roof. Yet Jesus, the One sent from God, wanted to dine with me. I scrambled down, my heart pounding like a drum. My feet could scarcely carry me as I welcomed Him with gladness.

The whispers rose around us. "He has gone to be the guest of a notorious sinner," they muttered. But their disapproval could not quench the fire kindled inside me.

That night, as we reclined at my table, I looked into His eyes, eyes full of mercy and truth. The weight of my greed, my lies, my betrayal of my people—it was all exposed, yet I did not feel condemned. I felt loved. And love transformed me.

I stood and declared before Him and my household, "I will give half my wealth to the poor, Lord. And if I have cheated people on their taxes, I will give them back four times as much!" My voice trembled, but it was steady with conviction.

Jesus' words still echo within me: "Salvation has come to this home today, for this man has shown himself to be a true son of Abraham. For the Son of Man came to seek and save those who are lost."

He was speaking of me—I was the lost one, and He sought me out, found me in a tree, and saved me in my own house.

Then Jesus leaned forward and spoke a parable that sank deep into our souls. He told us of a nobleman who was to travel to a distant land to be crowned king and then return. Before leaving, the nobleman called ten of his servants and entrusted each with money, instructing them to invest it faithfully until he returned.

Some servants took the gift seriously. When the nobleman returned, one had multiplied his share ten times over. The king said to him, "Well done! You are faithful. Because you have been trustworthy with a little, I will give you authority over ten cities." Another came, having multiplied his portion five times. Again, the king rewarded him, giving him authority over five cities.

But one servant came trembling. He had hidden the money in fear, doing nothing with what was entrusted to him. His excuse was that the nobleman was harsh, and so he had buried his share away. The king's response cut to the bone: "If you believed I was so harsh, why did you not at least put my money in the bank to earn interest?" The little he had was taken from him and given to the one who had proven most faithful.

Then Jesus' voice grew strong as He added that those who rejected the nobleman's rule altogether—those who said, "We do not want him to be our king"—were destroyed when the king returned.

As His words filled the room, I realized He was not simply speaking of money. He was teaching us that each of us has been entrusted with life, breath, influence, and opportunities for the Kingdom of God. The question was not how much we had been given, but whether we were faithful with it. Faithfulness would bring reward, but fear, laziness, or outright rejection of His reign would bring loss and judgment.

Sitting there, I understood something I had never seen before. My wealth, my power, my position—they were nothing compared to the treasure of His Kingdom. What mattered now was faithfulness to Him. No longer would I live to hoard and hide; I would live to invest everything—my life, my resources, my influence—for Jesus, the true King.

That night, my house became a place of joy. The same walls that once echoed with greed and emptiness now resounded with the hope of eternal life.

Scriptures: Luke 19:1-27

The Estate

I HAD BEEN WRESTLING with bitterness for months. Ever since my father passed, my brother and I had been at odds over his estate. Father's land—our inheritance—was supposed to bind us together, but instead it drove a wedge so deep between us that even our neighbors turned away, weary of hearing our quarrels.

I was the younger son, and by custom I deserved a portion, yet my brother held tightly to it all, claiming his rights as the firstborn. Day after day, I felt anger twist and grow within me. I wanted fairness. I wanted what belonged to me. But most of all, I wanted relief from the shame of being overlooked, as if my father's legacy did not matter in me.

Then I heard that Jesus was nearby, teaching the crowds. People spoke of His wisdom, His compassion, His authority like no other rabbi. They said He healed the sick, forgave sins, even cast out demons. In my desperation, I thought—surely, He will see justice, surely, He will command my brother to do what is right.

So I pushed through the crowd, my voice loud and raw, "Teacher, please tell my brother to divide our father's estate with me!"

I expected His agreement. Instead, His eyes pierced through me—not with anger, but with a knowing that unsettled my soul.

"Friend," He said gently, "who made me a judge over you to decide such things as that?"

The words stopped me cold. My mouth hung open, shame washing over me. Was He refusing me? Did He not care about my plight? Yet His voice carried deeper, reaching past the dispute to the very root of my heart.

"Beware! Guard against every kind of greed. Life is not measured by how much you own."

I felt as though He had torn away the layers of my frustration, exposing the truth I did not want to face. It was not just my brother's stubbornness—it was my own hunger for more, my own fixation on what I lacked rather than the God who provides.

He told a story then, about a rich man whose land produced so many crops that he decided to tear down his barns and build bigger ones. I listened intently, almost forgetting my brother's scowl beside me. The man in the parable congratulated himself, saying he would take it easy, eat, drink, and be merry. But God said to him, "You fool! You will die this very night. Then who will get everything you worked for?"

A chill ran through me. Was I any different? I thought my fight for inheritance was about justice, but really, it was about security, possessions, and the illusion of control.

Jesus went on to teach His disciples, but His words struck me too. He spoke of ravens that do not plant or harvest or store in barns, yet God feeds them. He pointed to the lilies, clothed in beauty without labor or thread, more glorious than Solomon in all his splendor.

"If God cares so wonderfully for flowers that are here today and thrown into the fire tomorrow," He said, "He will certainly care for you. Why do you have so little faith?"

His words pierced me deeper than my quarrel with my brother ever had. I had been clinging to inheritance as if my very life depended on it. But here was One telling me my Father in heaven knew all I needed before I even asked.

"Seek the Kingdom of God above all else, and he will give you everything you need."

My fists, which had been clenched for months, slowly loosened at my sides. My anger at my brother felt strangely small, my longing for fairness swallowed by something greater—an invitation to trust the God who already called me His son.

That day, I walked away still uncertain of how the inheritance would be divided, but certain of something greater: no earthly estate could compare to the treasure of belonging to Him.

Scriptures: Luke 12:13-34

The Banquet Invitation

THE AIR IN THE room was thick with the smell of roasted lamb and bread still warm from the fire. We were gathered in the home of a leading Pharisee, reclining at low tables, the couches filled with men of reputation—teachers of the Law, men of influence, and of course, Jesus Himself.

There was tension, as there always was around Him. Some listened with hungry hearts, others with sharp eyes, hoping to catch Him in error. Yet none could look away.

I watched Him closely. He saw what others missed. His gaze swept across the room, landing on the way men scrambled for seats of honor near the host. Then He began to speak, and His words fell like a plumb line straight through our pride:

"When you are invited to a wedding feast, don't sit in the seat of honor... take the lowest place... For those who exalt themselves will be humbled, and those who humble themselves will be exalted." (Luke 14:8–11 NLT)

A nervous shifting passed through the room. A knot tightened within me. His words cut deeper than mere table etiquette—they struck at the posture of my soul.

Then He turned to our host. His voice was steady, unflinching: "When you put on a luncheon or a banquet, don't invite your friends, brothers, relatives, and rich neighbors... Instead, invite the poor, the crippled, the lame, and the blind. Then at the resurrection of the righteous, God will reward you." (Luke 14:12–14 NLT)

Something welled up in me. The thought of such a feast—the poor, the broken, the forgotten sitting in honor—it stirred something I could not contain. Words leapt from my mouth before I could catch them:

"What a blessing it will be to attend a banquet in the Kingdom of God!"

The room fell silent. Jesus turned His eyes toward me, and I felt laid bare beneath His gaze. Then He told a story—one that burned its way into my heart.

A man prepared a great banquet. Invitations went out, but the guests made excuses. One had a field to tend. Another, oxen to try. Another had just married. They turned away from the feast for lesser things.

The master was furious. He sent his servants into the streets to bring in the poor, the crippled, the blind, and the lame. And still there was room. So he sent them further, into the roads and country lanes, to compel all to come until his house was full.

But Jesus was not finished. His voice grew heavier, more piercing. He spoke of a king who prepared a wedding feast for his son. Invitations went out, but again they were ignored, rejected, and even mocked. The king's fury burned hot, and judgment fell on those who scorned his kindness.

Then the king opened his doors wide—inviting everyone, good and bad alike, until the hall was full. Yet when he entered, he found one man not wearing wedding clothes. "Friend," he said, "how is it that you are here without wedding clothes?" The man was silent. He was bound hand and foot and cast out into darkness.

And then came the words that still echo in my soul: "For many are called, but few are chosen." (Matthew 22:14 NLT)

I sat frozen. My earlier words—"What a blessing it will be..."—sounded different now, weightier, sharper. To attend the banquet of God's Kingdom was indeed a blessing beyond imagination. But it was no casual thing. To come required more than a seat at the table—it required humility, surrender, and being clothed not in my own righteousness but in the covering only God could give.

My food grew cold before me. My appetite was gone. All I could think of was the King's invitation and my response. Would I be among the honored poor who came? Or would I cling to my excuses, my pride, my own garments—and be cast out?

Scriptures: Luke 14:7-24 and Matthew 22:1-14

The One

I HAD BARELY BEEN out of prison for a week. Three years behind stone walls and iron bars had hardened me in ways I didn't even understand yet. My crime wasn't noble, it wasn't a mistake—it was theft. I took what wasn't mine, and I paid the price. Even now, walking the streets again, I could still feel the stares burning into my back. Mothers pulled their children closer. Merchants kept an eye on their purses when I passed by. Shame clung to me like a shadow that wouldn't lift.

But that day, I heard a commotion down the road. People were hurrying, whispering a name I had heard so often even in prison—Jesus. Some of the men who were locked up with me had spoken of Him as if He were more than a rabbi, more than a prophet. They said He healed the sick, forgave sins, and ate with men like us. I didn't know if I believed it, but something in me ached to find out.

I followed the sound of the crowd until I saw Him standing in the middle of it all. A circle had formed, people pressing in from every side—merchants, farmers, beggars, women clutching children, even tax collectors. I recognized some of them, men I had seen at dice games, cheats I used to drink with. And there they were, leaning in close, unashamed.

But standing apart, robed and stiff, were the Pharisees. I knew their type well. Always watching. Always judging. Their lips curled as they whispered loud enough for us all to hear, "This man welcomes sinners and even eats with them."

My gut twisted. Their words pierced deep because they were true—I was a sinner. I deserved the scorn. But then Jesus spoke, and His voice cut through the tension, clear and steady, yet warm as firelight.

He told a story.

"If a man has a hundred sheep and one of them gets lost, what will he do? Won't he leave the ninety-nine others in the wilderness and go search for the one that is lost until he finds it?"

I pictured it in my mind—a shepherd at dusk, counting his flock, and then the sickening jolt when he realized one was missing. I could almost hear the wind whistling across the hills as he called out into the night. Every step he took away from the safety of the ninety-nine was a step deeper into danger, but still he went. Why? Because that one mattered.

And then Jesus said, "And when he has found it, he will joyfully carry it home on his shoulders."

The image pierced me—he didn't drag the sheep back, angry at its foolishness. He lifted it onto his shoulders with joy. Carried its weight as if it were treasure. My throat tightened. I had been that lost sheep wandering in the dark. And yet, no one ever came looking for me. Not family, not neighbors, not the priests. They were glad to see me gone, glad the trouble was out of sight. But here Jesus was saying God Himself would search for me. Would carry my weight, my shame, with joy.

Before I could untangle my thoughts, Jesus gave another picture.

"Or suppose a woman has ten silver coins and loses one. Won't she light a lamp and sweep the entire house and search carefully until she finds it?"

I saw her in my mind—hands shaking as she lit the lamp, the glow chasing away shadows. She moved everything, sweeping corners, bending low, refusing to give up until she found what was missing.

"And when she finds it, she will call in her friends and neighbors and say, 'Rejoice with me because I have found my lost coin.'"

I closed my eyes. A coin has no voice, no way to cry out. It can't find its way back on its own. It just lies there, forgotten in the dust—until someone decides it's too valuable to leave lost. That's what He was saying, wasn't it? That even when I had nothing to offer, God still searched for me. Yet in my darkest nights, no one searched. No one lit a lamp for me. I had been discarded, forgotten, like a coin left to rust. And now Jesus was saying heaven itself would celebrate if I were found.

Then He said something that sent a shiver through me: "In the same way, there is joy in the presence of God's angels when even one sinner repents."

Heaven rejoices... over one. Over me.

The Pharisees' faces grew darker with every word, but I couldn't look at them anymore. My gaze was fixed on Him. It was as if He were telling my story, peeling back every layer of guilt, exposing every failure, and yet offering something I never thought possible—love. Not the kind you earn, not the kind you bargain for, but the kind that finds you when you're still dirty and lost.

Then came the story that undid me—the father and the two sons.

Jesus spoke of the younger son who demanded his inheritance, ran off, and wasted it all on reckless living. Soon, famine struck, and the boy found himself starving, feeding pigs, wishing he could eat their slop. I swallowed hard. I knew that hunger. That emptiness. That filth. I had lived in my own pigsty, not of mud but of sin, and I had no one.

And what gripped me hardest was this—no one came looking for him. His brother didn't search the roads, his neighbors didn't rescue him. He was alone, broken, forgotten. Just like me in prison. Just like me in the nights when silence screamed louder than chains.

Yet as Jesus spoke, He revealed something else—when the son left, the father lost his son. Though he never stopped being a father, his heart ached with absence. Every day he waited, every day he watched the road, scanning the horizon, longing for the silhouette of the boy he loved. His heart was torn with grief, yet it never let go of hope. Broken, yet still loving. Wounded, yet still expectant.

But then Jesus' voice softened: "When he finally came to his senses, he said, 'I will go home to my father and say, "Father, I have sinned against both heaven and you, and I am no longer worthy of being called your son. Please take me on as a hired servant."'"

And while the son was still far down the road, his father saw him. Not because someone had gone after him. Not because he had fixed himself. But because the father was watching, waiting. And when he saw him, he ran.

I felt tears sting my eyes. The father didn't wait with arms crossed, demanding explanations. He sprinted, robes flapping, joy spilling out, and embraced his filthy, ruined son. The son tried to confess, but the father smothered him with love and called for a robe, a ring, sandals, and a feast.

I shook as the story settled into me. I had spent so long believing no one would ever come for me—and it was true, no one did. But Jesus was saying something greater: God Himself waits, God Himself runs, God Himself restores.

By the end, I knew. I was the lost sheep. I was the coin. I was the son. And He—this Jesus—was the one who came looking for me.

I pressed a hand against my chest, whispering into the noise, "I'm found."

And for the first time in years, I believed it.

Scripture: Luke 15:1–32

70 Times 7

I HAD BEEN CARRYING this question for days. Forgiveness was never easy for me. Growing up, my brother Andrew and I worked side by side as fishermen, and more than once we argued until our voices echoed across the water. I could forgive him once, maybe twice—but when the same offense happened again and again, the frustration built inside me. By the time I met Jesus, I thought I knew what was reasonable. Forgive a few times, then be done with it.

Among our rabbis, it was taught that if you forgave a man three times, you had done well, but the fourth time you were not obligated. That seemed fair to me. Even generous. So when I asked Jesus, I thought I would go beyond what was expected. "Lord, how often should I forgive someone who sins against me? Seven times?" I thought that would be more than enough. Seven was the number of completeness, the kind of answer that would sound holy.

Jesus turned toward me with that look that always pierced deeper than my words. "No, not seven times," He said, "but seventy times seven."

My mouth went dry. Seventy times seven? That wasn't just a number—it was a flood without banks, mercy without measure. I thought of our Scriptures, how Lamech once boasted in Genesis that if Cain was avenged seven times, then Lamech seventy-seven times. His words had been about vengeance without limit. Now here was Jesus, overturning that old curse, declaring that in His kingdom forgiveness would be without limit.

He said my name then, and I'll never forget it. "Peter, do you see? Forgiveness isn't about counting. It's about your heart. Just as the Father has forgiven you, you must forgive without measure."

His words went through me like a sharp wind. He wasn't just speaking to the crowd—He was speaking to me. Forgive without measure. Forgive as I have been forgiven.

Then He told us a story that cut me to the core.

A king wanted to settle accounts with his servants. One of them owed him an impossible sum—more than anyone could pay in ten lifetimes. The king ordered him to be sold, along with his family, but when the servant begged for mercy, the king forgave everything. The entire debt was wiped away.

But that same servant went out and found a man who owed him only a small amount. Instead of showing mercy, he grabbed him by the throat and demanded payment. When the man pleaded, he refused and threw him into prison.

When the king heard of it, he was furious. "You wicked servant! I forgave you that tremendous debt because you pleaded with me. Shouldn't you have mercy on your fellow servant, just as I had mercy on you?" The servant was thrown into prison until every last coin was paid.

Then Jesus looked at us and said, "That's what my heavenly Father will do to you if you refuse to forgive your brothers and sisters from your heart."

I shifted uncomfortably. My thoughts went to Andrew again, to the other disciples who sometimes wore on me, even to those who mocked us for following Jesus. Forgive from the heart? Always? My pride recoiled at it, yet something in me knew He was right. How could I hold on to grudges when God had shown me such mercy?

Later, He spoke about it again. "If another believer sins, rebuke that person; then if there is repentance, forgive. Even if that person wrongs you seven times a day and each time turns again and asks forgiveness, you must forgive."

Seven times in one day? My head spun. I muttered under my breath, "Who could do that?" and the others nodded with me. So we all said aloud, "Show us how to increase our faith!"

Jesus looked at me again. "Peter," He said softly, "you don't need more faith to forgive. You only need to trust the Father as much as a mustard seed. Forgive because you belong to Him, not because it is easy."

Then He spoke of servants. A servant doesn't expect thanks or reward for doing his duty. He simply obeys. In the same way, forgiveness isn't something extra we do to look holy—it's the life God expects of us.

That truth sank deep into me. Forgiveness wasn't about counting offenses or keeping score. It was about living free, the way God had set me free. It was about remembering the mountain of debt I could never repay, and how the Master had forgiven it all.

I looked at Andrew, at James and John, at all the faces around me, and I knew I would need this lesson more times than I could count. Forgiveness was not just His command—it was His gift.

Scriptures: Matthew 18:21-35, Luke 17:1-10

The Future

As we left the temple that day, I couldn't help but take in its beauty. The massive stones glowed in the afternoon light, each fitted with such precision that it seemed as though they would stand forever. I nodded, my gaze still on the massive structure. Then I turned to Jesus and said what was on all our minds: "Teacher, look at these remarkable buildings! Look at the size of these stones."

He looked at us with an expression that cut through all the wonder. His voice was steady, sure: "The time is coming when all these things will be completely demolished. Not one stone will be left on top of another."

His words struck me deeply. The temple—the center of our people, the place where God's presence had dwelled, where countless generations had offered sacrifices—gone? It was hard to grasp. Yet, I had learned never to dismiss His words. What He spoke always came with purpose.

Later, as we sat on the Mount of Olives across from the temple, the others and I drew closer to Him. The stones of the temple still shone in the fading light, a reminder of what He had just said. With James, John, and Andrew beside me, Andrew, with his eyes fixed on the walls leaned closer and whispered, "Go ahead, Peter—ask Him. You know we're all thinking it."

I asked, "Tell us, when will all this happen? What sign will show us that these things are about to be fulfilled?"

Even as we asked, I realized something was settling in among us. For so long, He had spoken of going away, of being rejected, of rising again. We never wanted to believe it. We hoped He meant something else. But now, with every word, it became clearer—He truly was preparing us for a time when He would not be with us in the way He was now. Our question about His return carried with it the dawning understanding that He would be leaving.

He began slowly, carefully, as though building something in us that would need to endure. "Don't let anyone mislead you. For many will come in my name, claiming, 'I am the Messiah.' They will deceive many. And you will hear of wars and threats of wars, but don't panic. Yes, these things must take place, but the end won't follow immediately. Nation will rise against nation, and kingdom against kingdom. There will be earthquakes in many parts of the world, as well as famines. But this is only the beginning—like the first pains before birth."

I felt the weight of it. Not fear, but clarity. The world as we knew it would not stay as it was.

Then He looked at us with unwavering seriousness. "You will be arrested, persecuted, and killed. You will be hated all over the world because you are my followers. But the Good News must first be preached to all nations. When you are arrested and stand trial, don't worry beforehand about what to say. Just say what God gives you at that time, for it will not be you speaking, but the Holy Spirit."

I listened closely. Arrests, trials, hatred—none of it sounded easy, but His words steadied me. The Spirit would be with us. Even in hardship, God Himself would not leave us.

Then He spoke of days of great distress: "A time is coming when you will see the sacrilegious object that causes desecration standing where it should not be. Then those in Judea must flee to the hills. A person on the roof must not go down into the house. A person in the field must not return even to get a coat. How terrible it will be for pregnant women and for nursing mothers in those days. And pray that your flight will not be in winter."

I set my hand against the stone beside me, steady much like the stones of the Temple. These were not words of despair—they were words to prepare us, to anchor us when the world shook apart.

He continued: "If anyone tells you, 'Look, here is the Messiah,' or, 'There He is,' don't believe it. For false messiahs and false prophets will rise up and perform signs and wonders to deceive, if possible, even God's chosen ones. See, I have told you ahead of time."

The shadows stretched long as He spoke of signs in the heavens: the sun growing dark, the moon failing to give its light, stars falling, powers in the heavens shaken. Then His voice carried hope like a steady flame: "Then everyone will see the Son of Man coming on the clouds with great power and glory. And He will send out His angels to gather His chosen ones from all over the world—from the farthest ends of the earth and heaven."

I breathed deeply. His return was certain. His glory would be revealed. That promise overshadowed the trials.

He continued, "When the Son of Man returns, it will be like it was in Noah's day. People were eating and drinking, marrying and giving in marriage, right up to the time Noah entered his boat. They lived as though nothing would ever change, ignoring the warnings of what was to come. Then the floodwaters rose suddenly and swept them all away. So it will be when the Son of Man comes. People will be caught in the middle of their ordinary routines—two men working together in the field; one will be taken, the other left. Two women grinding flour at the mill; one will be taken, the other left. Judgment will come swiftly, separating those who belong to Him from those who do not. So you also must keep watch, for you do not know the day or the hour."

Then He spoke of Lot, and I could see the firelight flicker in His eyes as He recalled it. "And the world will be as it was in the days of Lot. People went on with life as though nothing was wrong—eating and drinking, buying and selling, planting and building—until the very morning Lot left Sodom. Then fire and burning sulfur rained down from heaven and destroyed them all. Yes, it will be 'business as usual' right up to the day when the Son of Man is revealed. On that day, don't cling to the things of this world. A person on the roof must not go back into the house. A person in the field must not turn back. Remember Lot's wife! Whoever clings to their life will lose it, and whoever lets their life go will preserve it."

The weight of His words pressed into me. It wasn't only a warning of judgment—it was a call to live free from attachment to this world, to live ready for His appearing, knowing that when He returns, there will be no time to prepare. Only those already walking with Him will be gathered to Him.

The cool of the evening settled around us. His words demanded readiness, not speculation.

Then He spoke of faithfulness. "The servant who is faithful and wise, the one the master finds doing his work when he returns, will be rewarded. But if the servant says, 'My master won't be back for a while,' and begins to mistreat others, to drink and live carelessly, the master will return unexpectedly, and that servant will be cast out among the hypocrites. There, there will be weeping and gnashing of teeth."

His gaze lingered on each of us, not condemning, but searching. He was calling us to live steady, faithful, prepared.

I looked again at the temple glowing faintly in the moonlight. The stones looked immovable, yet He had said they would fall. I thought of my own life—my loyalty, my resolve. Would I remain firm when trials came, or waver like those swept away in Noah's day?

One thing was clear: I must stay watchful, ready, and faithful. For He would return again, and when He did, nothing else would matter.

Scriptures: Matthew 24:1-51, Mark 13:1-37, Luke 17:20-37

Bridesmaids

THE NIGHT HAD GROWN still when the Master told us another parable. His voice carried across the circle of disciples and followers, each word heavy with meaning.

"The Kingdom of Heaven will be like ten bridesmaids who took their lamps and went to meet the bridegroom," He said.

I leaned forward, the flicker of a nearby lamp reflecting in my eyes. Weddings had always stirred something deep in me. The waiting, the joy, the sudden arrival of the bridegroom—it was etched into the life of our people.

Later that night, as we walked away from the crowd, one of the others spoke quietly to me.

"Thaddeus," he said, "you seemed unsettled as He spoke. What were you thinking?"

I sighed, my thoughts still stirring. "Because I know our weddings," I answered. "After the betrothal, the bridegroom leaves for his father's house. He builds a place for her, and she never knows when he will return. Her whole life becomes a waiting, a readiness. The bridesmaids stay near, lamps prepared, their love and loyalty proved by their watchfulness. That is what He was showing us tonight."

My companion nodded, and we walked in silence for a moment, the gravel crunching underfoot. But I could not stop speaking, for the weight of it pressed on me. "Don't you see? All ten looked alike. They all dressed like bridesmaids. They all carried lamps. They all waited. But only half of them were truly ready. The others had nothing real within—no oil, no flame."

The Master's words replayed in my heart: "At midnight the cry rang out: 'Here comes the bridegroom!'" I could almost hear the shouts echoing through the night, see the frantic fumbling of the foolish ones, their empty lamps clattering in their hands.

I turned to my brother again. "It's not enough to look the part. The foolish begged for the door to open, but the bridegroom said, 'I don't know you.' That's what crushed me. To look like you belong, but to stand unknown when He comes..." My voice trailed off.

He laid a hand on my shoulder. "So it is about knowing Him."

"Yes," I whispered. "And being known by Him. The wise bridesmaids weren't just prepared out of duty. They were in love, longing for Him, their hearts burning with expectation. Everything they did in their waiting was shaped by Him, for Him. That is the oil. That is the flame."

We walked on in silence, the night wrapping around us. Above us, the stars stretched wide and uncountable. In my heart, His words kept burning: "So you, too, must keep watch! For you do not know the day or the hour of my return."

It is not about appearances. It is not about simply carrying a lamp. It is about knowing Him so deeply that my whole life becomes an offering of love, waiting with joy for the sound of His return.

Scriptures: Matthew 25:1–13

Triumphant Entry

THE ROAD INTO JERUSALEM that day was unlike anything I had ever seen. I was stationed along the route, one of many soldiers ordered to keep peace as pilgrims poured in for the feast. Normally, this time of year meant heightened tensions—crowds easily stirred, tempers quick to flare. Rome knew how fragile Jerusalem could be, and our presence was meant to remind them who held the power. But this was no ordinary entry.

I heard the commotion long before I saw its cause—cheers rising, voices shouting in unison, children running ahead with branches torn from the trees. The crowd surged like a wave, and in the middle of it all was a man riding a young donkey. Not a warhorse. Not a chariot. A donkey.

I could not help but think how strange it looked. Roman generals returned from conquest on white stallions, draped in armor, paraded with banners and trumpets. Here, this Jesus—yes, I had heard his name whispered for months—came low, unarmed, clothed like any other commoner. And yet the people treated him as if he were a king.

"Praise God for the Son of David!" they cried. "Blessings on the one who comes in the name of the Lord! Hail to the King of Israel!" The words rolled over me in languages I scarcely understood. Some threw cloaks across the road before him, as if to honor a victorious ruler. The sound of palm branches swishing through the air surrounded me.

I glanced at the Jewish leaders standing off to the side. Their faces were not joyful; they were twisted with anger. I caught fragments of their muttering—fear that all this commotion might draw Rome's wrath, jealousy that this man drew the praise they longed for. It struck me: the very ones who should have welcomed him as their own king seemed the most unsettled.

I tried to make sense of it all. To us Romans, power is shown through force, through fear, through triumph in battle. But here was a man, unarmed and gentle, receiving more honor than Caesar himself would from these people. How could humility carry such weight? What kind of kingdom comes without legions?

As he drew near, I caught sight of his face. He wasn't basking in their shouts like a man drunk on glory. No, there was something else—something deeper. His eyes, I swear, were filled with sorrow. At one moment he stopped, looking over the city, and I saw tears. He wept. Who weeps in the hour of their triumph?

"Jerusalem," he whispered, words I could barely catch, "how I wish today that you of all people would understand the way to peace. But now it is too late..."

Peace. That was not the Roman way. We enforced peace through blood and iron. But this man spoke of a peace beyond fear, and the crowd believed him. I could not shake the thought: perhaps he saw something we did not.

By the time he entered the city, the entire place was stirred. "Who is this man?" people kept asking. Some said prophet. Others said Messiah. To me, he was a mystery—one who defied everything I knew about power and authority.

I was just a soldier, sworn to Rome, but that day I realized I was witnessing something greater than any military triumph. I had seen men hail emperors, but never had I seen a man on a donkey draw the worship of thousands.

And I wondered—was this man truly a threat to Rome? Or was he a threat to something far deeper, something in the heart of every man?

Scriptures: Matthew 21:1-11, Mark 11:1-11, Luke 19:28-44, and John 12:12-19

The Fig Tree

I FOLLOWED CLOSE BEHIND Him that day as we entered Jerusalem. The city seemed to pulse with expectation—Passover pilgrims filling the streets, the air thick with prayers, laughter, and the cries of merchants selling doves and lambs. My heart beat fast. Just hours earlier, the people had laid down branches, shouting "Hosanna!" as if He were already crowned King. And yet, when we entered the Temple courts, He did not take a throne. He simply looked around. His eyes searched every corner, and though He said nothing, I could sense His grief. Evening shadows fell, and we returned to Bethany.

The next morning, hunger pressed against my ribs as we walked back toward the city. Jesus spotted a fig tree covered with leaves. I thought surely it would yield fruit for Him, but when He reached into the branches, there was nothing but emptiness. His voice, steady but heavy with authority, cut the silence: "May no one ever eat your fruit again!" (Mark 11:14 NLT).

The words startled me. Why curse a tree? I turned it over in my heart, wondering if He was showing us something far deeper than food.

We entered the Temple once more, and suddenly the quiet restraint of yesterday vanished. His righteous anger filled the courts as He drove out the money changers. The crack of overturned tables and the scattering of coins echoed off the stones. Doves fluttered, men shouted, children gasped. Yet His words carried greater weight than the chaos: "The Scriptures declare, 'My Temple will be called a house of prayer for all nations,' but you have turned it into a den of thieves." (Mark 11:17 NLT).

I felt conviction rise in me. This was not only about merchants and coins—it was about purity of heart. His voice carried the authority of heaven itself, and for a moment I saw the Temple as it was meant to be: a place for all nations to seek God.

That evening, as we left the city, my thoughts kept circling. Was He cleansing only the courts, or was He pointing to something within us that needed cleansing too?

The next morning, the fig tree we had passed was shriveled from the roots up. Peter gasped, and we all stared. It was no ordinary withering—it was as though life had been cut off in an instant. The tree had looked so full, yet it bore no fruit. Was this what we would become if we carried only the appearance of life without truly believing?

Jesus turned to us, His eyes clear and searching. "Have faith in God. I tell you the truth, you can say to this mountain, 'May you be lifted up and thrown into the sea,' and it will happen. But you must really believe it will happen and have no doubt in your heart. I tell you, you can pray for anything, and if you believe that you've received it, it will be yours. But when you are praying, first forgive anyone you are holding a grudge against, so that your Father in heaven will forgive your sins, too." (Mark 11:22–25 NLT).

I wanted to believe. Yet I knew my own doubts. His words pierced me deeper still. Forgive? That struck a raw place in me. Forgiveness was never easy, and yet He spoke as if prayer itself depended on it.

As we walked on, my steps slowed. Faith that moved mountains... forgiveness that opened heaven's doors. I wrestled within myself. Could I really believe like that? Could I forgive like that?

Still, I knew this: His words were true. His authority was not just over trees and temples, but over hearts—mine included. And though doubt stirred within me, something stronger whispered: "Trust Him, Thomas. Trust Him."

Scriptures: Mark 11:11-26, Matthew 21:12-22

Temple Courtyard

THAT MORNING HAD BEGUN like so many others in Jerusalem. The temple courts bustled with pilgrims, the smell of incense drifted on the air, and we Pharisees had already gathered in the chambers along the portico. We debated matters of the law, sharpened our questions, and whispered of the Galilean who troubled us all. His name came up again and again. Jesus. He had overturned tables just the day before, His voice thundering through the courts: "My Temple will be called a house of prayer, but you have turned it into a den of thieves!"

I burned inside at the memory. Who was He to rebuke us in our own house? Yet word reached us quickly—He was back. He was teaching in the courtyard again, surrounded by a throng that hung on His every word. We could not ignore Him. Together, some of us priests, scribes, and Pharisees made our way toward the crowd.

I stood near the front, robes gathered in dignity, though my heart beat faster than I liked to admit. He looked straight through us, it seemed, as He began to tell a story.

"A man planted a vineyard, built a wall around it, dug a pit for pressing out the grape juice, and built a watchtower. Then he leased the vineyard to tenant farmers and moved to another country."

My stomach tightened. Isaiah's song of the vineyard flashed in my mind—Israel was the vineyard of the Lord. Every scholar of the law knew it. But Jesus wasn't finished.

"At the time of the grape harvest, the owner sent his servants to collect his share of the crop. But the farmers beat one, insulted another, killed another. Again and again the owner sent servants, but they were beaten, humiliated, or murdered."

I shifted uneasily. My eyes flicked toward the others standing beside me. We all knew what He was saying. These "servants" were the prophets our fathers had rejected. Was He daring to accuse us of carrying their same bloodstained legacy?

Then His voice lowered, weighty, every word like a hammer striking stone.

"Finally, the owner sent his son, whom he loved dearly. Surely they will respect my son, he thought. But the tenant farmers said, 'Here comes the heir to this estate. Let's kill him and take it for ourselves!' So they murdered him and threw his body out of the vineyard."

The people gasped. And in a flash, it was clear. He was speaking of Himself. He was saying we—the holy leaders of Israel—were the wicked farmers. Murderers. Thieves. Unworthy of the vineyard.

I felt the blood rush to my face. My hands trembled beneath my robe. How dare He! How dare He stand here and accuse us in front of this mob! Yet deep within, a sickening weight pressed against my chest, for I knew He spoke truth. We despised Him. We had already begun plotting His death.

Jesus' eyes burned as He looked straight at us, His voice sharp as a sword:

"What do you suppose the owner of the vineyard will do? I tell you—He will come, destroy those wicked tenants, and give the vineyard to others."

"No!" some in the crowd cried. But He only fixed His gaze and declared, "The stone that the builders rejected has now become the cornerstone. This is the Lord's doing, and it is wonderful to see."

His words cut deeper than any blade. The Scriptures we cherished, turned against us. And we realized—He meant us. We were the builders rejecting the stone. We were the tenants who would kill the heir.

Fury boiled inside me, yet so did fear. Every part of me wanted to seize Him, to silence Him forever. But the crowd was still there, hanging on His words, eyes filled with awe. If we moved against Him now, they would turn on us.

So I stood there, fists clenched beneath my robe, forcing my face to remain calm, though my insides twisted. His parable had unmasked us. His words had stripped away the pretense. We were the wicked farmers. And I hated Him for it.

But later, when I tried to sleep, His voice still echoed in the silence of my chamber:

"The stone the builders rejected has now become the cornerstone."

Scriptures: Matthew 21:33–46, Mark 12:1–12, and Luke 20:9–19

Final Week

The Helper

THE AIR IN THE room felt heavy, every word from His mouth pressing deep into us. We sat close around Him, the lamplight flickering on His face, shadows stretching across the walls. I drew nearer in thought, straining to catch every sound, though my heart struggled to grasp what He was preparing us for.

He told us these things so we would not abandon our faith when trials came. "For you will be expelled from the synagogues," He said, His voice firm, yet filled with sorrow. A hush fell over me as He continued, "The time is coming when those who kill you will think they are doing a holy service for God."

Matthew shifted beside me and whispered, "James... how can this be God's plan?"

I swallowed hard, keeping my eyes on Jesus. "I don't know, but His words carry truth. We must trust Him, even when we don't fully understand yet."

I felt my stomach twist. To be rejected by our own people, to be hunted, even killed? I looked at Peter across the table, his brow furrowed, his hands clenched. We all shifted uncomfortably, for we knew He wasn't exaggerating. The seriousness in His eyes told us this was no parable—this was our future.

Yet He went on, reminding us that those who did such things never truly knew the Father or Him. He said these words now, so when the hour came we would remember He had prepared us.

Still, my heart ached when He said, "None of you are asking where I am going. Instead, you grieve because of what I've told you." It was true. My spirit was heavy with sadness, unable to see past His leaving. But then He said something that puzzled me, something that sparked both hope and confusion: "It is best for you that I go away, because if I don't, the Advocate won't come. If I do go away, then I will send Him to you."

The Advocate? The Helper? My brother John and I exchanged glances. We whispered questions among ourselves, not daring to interrupt Him. He spoke of the Spirit convicting the world of sin, of God's righteousness, and of the coming judgment. He said the ruler of this world had already been judged. His words carried such authority, as though the verdict was already sealed.

But then He looked at us tenderly. "There is so much more I want to tell you, but you can't bear it now." I longed to know, to understand, but I knew He was right. We were already overwhelmed. He promised, "When the Spirit of truth comes, He will guide you into all truth. He will not speak on His own but will tell you what He has heard. He will tell you about the future. He will bring Me glory by telling you whatever He receives from Me."

I could not fully grasp it then, but there was comfort in knowing He would not leave us abandoned.

Still, His words about leaving pierced me deeply. "In a little while you won't see Me anymore. But a little while after that, you will see Me again." We murmured among ourselves. What could this mean? "What does He mean by 'a little while'?" I whispered to John. None of us understood.

But Jesus knew our thoughts, and He said plainly, "I tell you the truth, you will weep and mourn over what is going to happen to Me, but the world will rejoice. You will grieve, but your grief will suddenly turn to wonderful joy." He likened it to a woman giving birth—her anguish replaced by joy when her child is born.

His words sank into me like seeds waiting for their time. I couldn't see the full picture, yet something in His tone gave me hope. He spoke of the day when we would ask in His name, when the Father Himself would hear us because He loved us, because we believed He came from God.

And then, with such clarity, He said, "Yes, I came from the Father into the world, and now I will leave the world and return to the Father."

We nodded, relieved for a moment that He was speaking so plainly. "At last you are speaking clearly," we said. "Now we understand that You know everything, and there's no need to question You. From this we believe You came from God."

But He shook His head gently, "Do you finally believe? But the time is coming—indeed it's here now—when you will be scattered, each one going his own way, leaving Me alone. Yet I am not alone, because the Father is with Me."

Those words stung. To think that we, His closest friends, would abandon Him. My throat tightened, and my eyes welled with tears.

Then He gave us words I have carried in the deepest part of me ever since: "I have told you all this so that you may have peace in Me. Here on earth you will have many trials and sorrows. But take heart, because I have overcome the world."

Peace. In Him. Trials would come. Sorrows would press hard. But He—our Teacher, our Lord, our Friend—had already overcome.

As I sat there in the glow of the lamplight, His words pressed into me like fire upon my soul. I did not yet see the cross, nor the empty tomb, but those words carved hope into the deepest part of my being. I knew, no matter what came, His victory was already certain.

Scriptures: John 16:1-33

The Leper

I STILL REMEMBER THE day my world changed. My skin had long been marked with sores, my body disfigured, and my life exiled. Leprosy had stolen everything—family, friends, dignity, even the simple joy of walking freely into a marketplace. I was no longer Simon the craftsman, the neighbor, the son. I was Simon the leper, untouchable, a warning sign to anyone who dared come too close.

I had heard whispers of a man named Jesus, a healer who touched the broken and lifted the forgotten. I had seen others come back cleansed, their faces radiant, their lives restored. Still, I doubted if such mercy could reach me.

One morning, I decided I could not remain hidden in the shadows any longer. I made my way through a crowd that recoiled at my presence. Fear and shame pressed against me as much as their stares. Yet, there He was—Jesus of Nazareth, His gaze steady, His steps unhurried, as if He had been expecting me.

I fell at His feet, trembling. "Lord, if you are willing, you can make me clean."

He did not step back as so many had. Instead, He stretched out His hand and touched me. His hand, warm and firm, rested on what others called defiled. "I am willing. Be healed!" At that moment, the decay that had imprisoned me dissolved. My skin was renewed, but more than that—my soul felt alive again. He had given me back more than health; He had restored my place in the world, in my family, in God's mercy.

Now years later, I sit in my own home, a man no longer known for his disease but for the mercy I had received. Jesus reclined at my table, His disciples around Him. The house hummed with conversation and the fragrance of food. I marveled again that He would sit here, in my home, eating bread where once people would not even cross my threshold.

Then she entered—Mary, her steps quiet but full of intent. In her hands she carried an alabaster jar, sealed, precious. Without hesitation, she broke it open, and the room filled with the rich fragrance of pure nard. Its sweetness pressed into every corner, clinging to the air, saturating even the walls. She poured it upon His head, and then His feet, wiping them with her hair. It was an act so extravagant, so tender, that I felt the sting of tears in my eyes.

The murmurs began quickly. "Why waste such a costly perfume? It could have been sold and the money given to the poor." I glanced at Judas, whose words dripped with scorn, though his eyes flickered with something darker—greed, perhaps, or betrayal waiting for its moment.

But Jesus, calm and unshaken, defended her. "Leave her alone. She has done this in preparation for my burial. You will always have the poor among you, but you will not always have me." His words cut through the noise like a blade. Burial? The thought chilled me. How could this man who had brought life to me, to so many others, speak of death? Yet, His tone carried the weight of inevitability, as though He already bore the shadows of what was coming.

I leaned back, my mind wrestling. He had healed me with a touch, restored my life with a word, and here He was, speaking as if His own end was near. The perfume still lingered, its aroma now mingled with a heaviness that settled over my soul.

Later, I would hear whispers that Judas had slipped away to strike a bargain with the chief priests, selling his loyalty for silver. The religious leaders, hungry for a way to seize Jesus quietly, found their willing accomplice. The timing was cunning—they plotted even as the Passover drew near, a feast meant to remind us of deliverance.

And here I sat, a man once dead in shame and now alive because of Him, trying to understand how the Deliverer Himself would be given over.

I could not push away the thought: the same mercy that reached into my ruin would soon reach further still—through suffering, through blood, through a sacrifice I could hardly comprehend.

The fragrance of that broken jar lingered long after Mary left, a reminder that love, poured out fully, is never wasted.

Scriptures: Matthew 26:1-16, Mark 14:1-11, Luke 22:1-6

Love Knelt

THE ROOM WAS QUIET, filled with the familiar creak of wood as we reclined around the table. The meal had been prepared, and yet the air was heavy—different from any other night we had shared. Something in the way the Teacher moved, something in His eyes, told me this was no ordinary evening.

I watched as He rose from His place. He laid aside His robe and wrapped a towel around His waist. My mind raced—what was He doing? My Master, the One I had seen heal the blind and command storms to cease, was now filling a basin with water. The sound of the water pouring struck me strangely, echoing in my thoughts.

Then He began—stooping low to kneel, washing the dust from the feet of my brothers. The room fell into stunned silence. None of us moved. None of us dared to speak. We just watched Him—our Lord—take the posture of a servant. How could He?

I could hardly bear it as He drew closer. Andrew's eyes met mine, wide and searching, but neither of us spoke. I felt heat rise within me. This was not right. He should not be the one kneeling with a towel in His hands.

Then He came to me. My stomach churned, and the words burst out before I could stop them: "Lord, are you going to wash my feet?"

He looked at me—steady, calm, yet piercing. "Peter, you don't understand now what I am doing, but someday you will."

I shook my head. "No," I said, my voice firm, though inside I was trembling. "You will never ever wash my feet!" How could I let Him? He was the Messiah! It felt backwards, upside down. He should be exalted, not bending low before me.

His reply cut deep, yet it was filled with authority and love: "Unless I wash you, you won't belong to me."

The words stung my soul. Belong to Him? Could I lose that? My mind spun. I wanted Him—I needed Him. Every part of me ached to be His. If this was what it meant, then I wanted all of it. "Then wash my hands and head as well, Lord—not just my feet!"

A faint smile touched His face as He answered, "A person who has bathed all over does not need to wash, except for the feet, to be entirely clean. And you disciples are clean—but not all of you."

The way His voice lingered on those last words sent a chill through me. I looked around at the others. None of us moved. His eyes swept the room, steady and knowing. My thoughts turned quickly to Judas. There had been whispers among us, questions about his dealings. I had noticed the way his hand lingered a little too long on the moneybag, his glances that seemed distracted, troubled. Still, I wanted to push the thought away. Surely not one of us. Surely not him.

But when Jesus spoke, it was as if He already saw the road Judas had chosen. A shadow seemed to pass across Judas' face, though he tried to hide it. My heart grew heavy, torn between confusion and sorrow. I did not yet understand all that was unfolding, but I could feel it—this was not just about dirty feet. This was about the state of our souls. Clean, yet not all. It was not dirt on Judas' feet that condemned him, but the darkness he clung to in his heart. Only those who let Jesus wash them fully, inside and out, truly belong to Him.

When He had finished, He put His robe back on and sat down with us again. His voice carried both gentleness and weight: "Do you understand what I was doing? You call me 'Teacher' and 'Lord,' and you are right, because that's what I am. And since I, your Lord and Teacher, have washed your feet, you ought to wash each other's feet. I have given you an example to follow. Do as I have done to you. I tell you the truth, slaves are not greater than their master. Nor is the messenger more important than the one who sends the message. Now that you know these things, God will bless you for doing them."

I sat in silence, the towel still in my mind, the touch of His hands still vivid. My pride had resisted Him, but He had shown me something greater—that true greatness is found in humility. That night I realized: to belong to Him is to let Him serve me, and to learn from Him how to serve others.

Scriptures: John 13:1-17

The Lamb

THE UPPER ROOM WAS filled with the glow of oil lamps, their flickering light casting shadows across the walls. We had celebrated Passover many times before, but this night carried a weight unlike any other. I sat close beside Him, near enough to hear His voice as He spoke with an intensity I had never known.

"I have been very eager to eat this Passover meal with you before my suffering begins." The words stilled the room. Peter leaned toward me and whispered, "John, do you hear Him? It's as though everything has been leading to this night." He was right.

He took the bread, gave thanks, and broke it. The crack echoed through the room, louder than it should have been. "This is my body, given for you. Do this to remember me." We froze in awe. Nathaniel mouthed the words under his breath, as though carving them into his soul. Matthew's eyes widened, and even Peter, always so quick to speak, sat speechless. I held the bread in trembling hands, knowing this was more than symbol.

Then He lifted the cup, the firelight shimmering in the deep red surface. "This cup is the new covenant between God and his people—confirmed with my blood, which is poured out as a sacrifice for you." My spirit shook inside me. All those years of blood on doorframes, lambs sacrificed, altars drenched—all of it was pointing here. He wasn't just walking us through the steps of a Passover. He was showing us that He was the Lamb. This was real. The sacrifice was Him.

But then His voice grew heavy. He looked around the table and said, "I tell you the truth, one of you will betray me." The words cut through the room like a blade. We looked at one another, stunned. Whispers broke out. "Surely not me... Lord, is it I?" Fear and confusion rippled around the table.

Peter motioned toward me, his eyes urgent. "Ask Him who He means," He whispered. I drew close beside Jesus and asked quietly, "Lord, who is it?"

He replied softly, "It is the one to whom I give the bread I dip in the bowl." He dipped a piece of bread and handed it to Judas, son of Simon Iscariot. Judas' face went pale, his eyes darting away. Then Jesus looked at him and said, "Hurry and do what you're going to do."

Some of us thought He meant Judas should buy food for the festival or give something to the poor, but I saw something deeper in the Master's eyes—pain, yet also resolve. Judas took the bread, stood quickly, and slipped into the night. The door closed behind him, and the darkness seemed to swallow him whole.

The table remained still, each of us stunned, yet the weight of what Jesus had given us pressed deeper into me. The lamb on the table was only a shadow. The true Lamb was here, giving Himself for us. We had remembered the story of Egypt every year, but tonight the story had come alive before our eyes. The sacrifice was not tradition. It was Him.

When His gaze fell on me again, I felt seen to the depths—my strengths, my failings, my devotion, and even my weakness yet to come. Still His eyes held only love. That love, stronger than betrayal, stronger than death, is what has never left me.

Scriptures: Matthew 26:17–30, Mark 14:12–26, Luke 22:7–38, John 13

The Way, Truth, and Life

THE WEIGHT OF THE supper still lingered in the air. The bread, the cup, His words about betrayal and leaving us—it all pressed in like a storm cloud heavy with rain. My thoughts churned, unable to settle. I tried to hold His promises close, but they slipped through my mind like sand through open hands.

Jesus looked at us with such tenderness, as though He could see the tremors running through our souls. His voice steadied the room: "Don't let your hearts be troubled. Trust in God, and trust also in me. There is more than enough room in my Father's home. If this were not so, would I have told you that I am going to prepare a place for you? When everything is ready, I will come and get you, so that you will always be with me where I am. And you know the way to where I am going."

The others sat in silence, their faces etched with worry. I felt the weight of His words pressing deep within, stirring both longing and confusion. My lips burned with the question I couldn't hold back any longer.

"Thomas," one of the others whispered, sensing my struggle, "say what you are thinking."

So I did. My voice broke the heavy quiet: "No, we don't know, Lord. We have no idea where you are going, so how can we know the way?"

The room shifted. Eyes turned toward me, some with surprise, some perhaps relieved that I had spoken aloud what they dared not say. But He—He looked right at me. There was no frustration in His gaze, only a piercing love that seemed to search the deepest part of me.

"I am the way, the truth, and the life," He said. "No one can come to the Father except through me. If you had really known me, you would know who my Father is. From now on, you do know him and have seen him."

His words struck me like a sudden light in darkness. The way was not a road to travel or a secret path to discover. The way was Him. The truth was Him. The life was Him. I had asked for direction, and He gave Himself.

Philip spoke then, asking to see the Father, but Jesus answered with firmness: "Anyone who has seen me has seen the Father." His voice carried authority no man could counterfeit. He reminded us that His words and works were the Father's, flowing through Him. He spoke of us doing even greater works, of prayers answered in His name, of power that would come when He returned to the Father.

I hung on His words as He spoke of love. Not the shallow kind men often speak of, but love proven by obedience. "If you love me, obey my commandments. And I will ask the Father, and he will give you another Advocate, who will never leave you. He is the Holy Spirit, who leads into all truth."

The Holy Spirit. I had heard those words before in the Scriptures, in the stories of our fathers, but never with such closeness. The Spirit of God had come upon prophets, upon kings, upon judges of old—but Jesus spoke of Him not as a fleeting presence, but as One who would live with us and within us.

He would not be distant. He would not depart. He would guide us into truth, comfort us in sorrow, strengthen us when we faltered, remind us of all that Jesus had spoken. The very breath of God, dwelling not in a temple of stone, but in fragile men like us.

I could hardly grasp it. The thought of His Spirit resting on me felt both wondrous and impossible. Yet as Jesus spoke, a fire stirred deep within—a hope that what He promised would indeed come.

Judas—not Iscariot—asked why He would reveal Himself to us and not to the world, and Jesus answered with gentle clarity: His presence dwells with those who love Him, those who walk in obedience.

Then came the gift that even now I cling to: "I am leaving you with a gift—peace of mind and heart. And the peace I give is a gift the world cannot give. So don't be troubled or afraid."

Peace. Not the fragile kind the world offers, but peace born of His presence. Peace that would remain even when storms raged, even when our world fell apart.

He spoke of leaving, of returning, of His obedience to the Father's will. Each word pulled us closer to the edge of a mystery greater than our minds could hold. My question had opened the door for Him to unveil a truth that would change me forever.

That night, I realized something: my doubt had not driven Him away. My confusion had not silenced His love. Instead, my question became the very place He declared who He is. He is the way I longed to find, the truth my soul craved, the life I desperately needed.

And though my heart still wrestled with fear, His promise of the Spirit and His gift of peace rested upon me like a mantle I could not earn but only receive.

Scriptures: John 14:1-31

His Prayer

THE NIGHT WAS HEAVY with meaning. We had shared the meal with Him, heard His words of comfort and warning, and now His voice lifted toward heaven. My brother James said quietly, "John, come and sit by me." I came and sat beside him, and together we focused our attention on the Master. I remember every word as if it were carved into me, for His prayer was unlike anything I had ever heard before.

He looked up and said, "Father, the hour has come. Glorify your Son so he can give glory back to you. For you have given him authority over everyone. He gives eternal life to each one you have given him. And this is the way to have eternal life—to know you, the only true God, and Jesus Christ, the one you sent to earth. I brought glory to you here on earth by completing the work you gave me to do. Now, Father, bring me into the glory we shared before the world began" (John 17:1-5 NLT).

His words carried such weight. My thoughts spun at the mention of glory He had before the world existed. I knew Him as the man who called me by the seashore, but here He prayed as the eternal Son.

Then His voice softened as He spoke of us—those of us sitting near Him. "I have revealed you to the ones you gave me from this world. They were always yours. You gave them to me, and they have kept your word. Now they know that everything I have is a gift from you, for I have passed on to them the message you gave me. They accepted it and know that I came from you, and they believe you sent me" (John 17:6-8 NLT).

I glanced around at my brothers, knowing He was speaking of us. He was lifting us to His Father, cherishing the bond we shared with Him.

"I am praying for them. I am not praying for the world, but for those you have given me, because they belong to you. All who are mine belong to you, and you have given them to me, so they bring me glory. Now I am departing from the world; they are staying in this world, but I am coming to you. Holy Father, you have given me your name; now protect them by the power of your name so that they will be united just as we are" (John 17:9-11 NLT).

The word "protect" gripped me. I recalled how He had shielded us again and again—when crowds pressed too close, when storms raged on the sea, when religious leaders plotted His death. He guarded us, body and soul. And now He asked the Father to keep us safe in His name, safe in unity.

He went on, "During my time here, I protected them by the power of the name you gave me. I guarded them so that not one was lost, except the one headed for destruction, as the Scriptures foretold. Now I am coming to you. I told them many things while

I was with them in this world so they would be filled with my joy. I have given them your word. And the world hates them because they do not belong to the world, just as I do not belong to the world. I'm not asking you to take them out of the world, but to keep them safe from the evil one. They do not belong to this world any more than I do. Make them holy by your truth; teach them your word, which is truth" (John 17:12-17 NLT).

When He prayed that we would be holy by His truth, I felt the weight of His mission. He was setting us apart, not for escape, but for purpose.

Then His prayer reached further, beyond us who sat with Him that night. "Just as you sent me into the world, I am sending them into the world. And I give myself as a holy sacrifice for them so they can be made holy by your truth. I am praying not only for these disciples but also for all who will ever believe in me through their message" (John 17:18-20 NLT).

I could hardly take in the scope of it—He was praying for future believers, generations yet unborn, all who would come to know Him through the words He planted in us. That prayer stretched across time, binding us all together.

His voice grew stronger, full of longing. "I pray that they will all be one, just as you and I are one—as you are in me, Father, and I am in you. And may they be in us so that the world will believe you sent me. I have given them the glory you gave me, so they may be one as we are one. I am in them and you are in me. May they experience such perfect unity that the world will know that you

sent me and that you love them as much as you love me"
(John 17:21-23 NLT).

Unity. That was His heart. Not shallow agreement, but one-ness rooted in His very being. The kind of unity that would reveal the Father's love to the world. As He spoke, I realized this was no casual wish—it was His deepest desire.

He ended with this longing: "Father, I want these whom you have given me to be with me where I am. Then they can see all the glory you gave me because you loved me even before the world began! O righteous Father, the world doesn't know you, but I do; and these disciples know you sent me. I have revealed you to them, and I will continue to do so. Then your love for me will be in them, and I will be in them" (John 17:24-26 NLT).

When His words fell silent, the air itself seemed charged with love. He had prayed for us, for His mission, for the Father's glory, and for all who would ever believe. His heart burned with unity, love, and eternal hope.

Even now, those words echo inside me. That night was not only about us—it was about every soul He came to save. He prayed for me, for us, and all those yet to come.

Scriptures: John 17 1-26

Three Times

WHEN WE FINISHED THE meal, we lifted our voices together in song. It felt almost strange to worship there at the table, with the taste of bread and wine still fresh on my tongue, but at the same time it was beautiful. Our voices weren't perfect, but they were honest, carrying words of praise to the God of Israel who had delivered our ancestors long ago. The room filled with that sound, and for a moment, I wished it could always stay that way—Jesus with us, joy filling our hearts, hope alive in the song.

Then we stood and followed Him out into the cool night air, heading toward the Mount of Olives. I walked close, determined to stay near Him. He had just spoken words that still clung to me like heavy chains—about betrayal, about leaving us, about His time drawing near. Every step we took, I felt the weight of it pressing more firmly into my soul.

As we walked, He looked at us with eyes that seemed to see through the darkness of the night and into the darkness of what was to come. "Dear children," He said, His voice tender, almost like a father or an older brother preparing to leave us behind. "I will be with you only a little longer. So now I am giving you a new commandment: Love each other. Just as I have loved you, you should love each other. Your love for one another will prove to the world that you are my disciples."

I could hear John draw in a breath beside me. His words cut straight through us, simple yet piercing. Love one another. That was what mattered most to Him in these final hours. Not power. Not position. Not proving ourselves right. Love.

But His tone carried such urgency, as if He were trying to press these truths into our hearts before they shattered. I couldn't shake the thought—He knew. He knew exactly what was coming.

Then He turned His gaze directly to me. "Simon, Simon, Satan has asked to sift each of you like wheat. But I have pleaded in prayer for you, Simon, that your faith should not fail. So when you have repented and turned to me again, strengthen your brothers."

The words made my stomach twist. Satan—wanting to crush us, to scatter us like grain thrown to the wind. And yet Jesus was already praying for me. I swallowed hard, my pride rising to meet my fear. "Lord, I am ready to go to prison with you, and even to die with you!" I said it with all the boldness I could muster. I meant it—I truly did.

But His reply pierced me like a blade. "Peter, let me tell you something. Before the rooster crows tomorrow morning, you will deny three times that you even know me."

I stopped walking, stunned. My mouth opened to argue, but the words caught in my throat. Deny Him? Me? After everything?

No, it couldn't be. "Even if everyone else deserts you," I insisted, forcing the words out, "I never will."

He looked at me with such sorrow, not anger, not frustration—sorrow. As if He knew me better than I knew myself.

The others chimed in quickly, echoing my resolve. "We will never desert you either," they said. But in my heart, His words echoed louder than their promises.

The night seemed heavier now, every step toward the Mount pressing deeper into the unknown. He had called us children. He had begged us to love. He had warned us of what lay ahead. These were not the careless words of a teacher casually dismissing His students. They were the final words of a Shepherd, pouring out His heart for His flock before the wolves circled in.

I wanted to believe my strength would hold, that my courage was enough. But even as I spoke bold words, I could not shake the weight of His gaze, nor the sadness in His voice.

We walked on in silence, the sound of our earlier song fading into memory.

Scriptures: Matthew 26:31-35, Mark 14:27-31, Luke 22:31-38, John 13:31-38

The Garden

We followed Him across the valley, the full moon casting long shadows as we walked the familiar path toward the Mount of Olives. My feet were heavy, but not from the climb. It was the weight in His voice earlier that night, the way He spoke of His time being near, the way He called us "dear children" at the supper table. It still rang inside me. He had prayed for us, pleaded that we might be one. Now, we were crossing over to a garden He often went to—a place He knew well.

When we reached the grove, He told most of the brothers to stay near the entrance, but He took James, John, and me deeper into the shadows. I can still hear Him say, "My soul is crushed with grief to the point of death. Stay here and keep watch with Me." His words pierced me, but the night was heavy and my body was weary. Still, I nodded, determined not to fail Him.

He went a little farther and fell to the ground. I could faintly hear Him pray, "Father, if You are willing, please take this cup of suffering away from Me. Yet I want Your will to be done, not Mine." The sound of His cry shook me, but even then my eyes grew heavy. Sleep stole over me again and again, though I tried to resist. Each time He returned and found us sleeping, my face burned with shame. Once He said to me directly, "Simon, are you asleep? Couldn't you watch with Me even one hour? Keep watch and pray, so that you will not give in to temptation. For the spirit is willing, but the body is weak." I dropped my head, unable to answer.

The third time He returned, He stood taller, His face set. There was strength in His steps, as if heaven itself had sent Him help. "The time has come," He said. "The Son of Man is betrayed into the hands of sinners. Get up, let's go. Look, My betrayer is here!"

Torches and lanterns soon broke through the darkness. A crowd pressed into the garden, soldiers armed with swords and clubs, priests, and temple guards. Leading them was Judas, one of our own. I will never forget that moment. He stepped forward and greeted Jesus with a kiss, as if nothing were wrong. My blood boiled. Betrayal like that cut deeper than any blade.

Jesus, calm even in that hour, said to them, "Who are you looking for?" They answered, "Jesus the Nazarene." When He said, "I am He," the power of His words knocked them backward to the ground. I thought this was our moment—surely now the Kingdom would come.

When they stood again, they moved to seize Him. Rage surged in me. I drew my sword without thinking and swung with all my might. The high priest's servant, Malchus, cried out as my blade struck, severing his ear. I was ready to fight them all, ready to die with Him.

But Jesus stopped me. His voice was firm yet filled with love: "Peter put your sword back into its sheath. Shall I not drink from the cup of suffering the Father has given Me? Don't you realize I could ask My Father for thousands of angels to protect us, and He would send them instantly? But if I did, how would the Scriptures be fulfilled that describe what must happen now?"

Then He reached out and healed the servant's ear right in front of us all. The same hands that had washed my feet just hours before now touched His enemy and restored him. I stood frozen. His ways were not my ways.

The soldiers closed in, binding Him as though He were some dangerous criminal. He said to them, "Am I a dangerous revolutionary, that you come with swords and clubs to arrest Me? Why didn't you arrest Me in the Temple? I was there every day. But this is your moment, the time when the power of darkness reigns."

The weight of His words, the sight of His chains—it broke me. Fear gripped us all, and though I had boasted earlier that I would never leave Him, in that moment, we fled into the night. My feet carried me away even as my heart screamed to stay.

Scriptures: Matthew 26:36-56, Mark 14:32-52, Luke 22:39-53, John 18:1-11

The Denial

THEY DRAGGED JESUS AWAY into the night, ropes binding His hands as if He were some dangerous criminal. My feet moved almost against my will. Fear clawed at me, but I couldn't let Him out of my sight. Another disciple, one who was known to the high priest, went inside with Him. I stood at the outer gate, uncertain, until that disciple spoke to the servant girl and she let me in.

The courtyard was alive with firelight and shadows. The smell of burning wood mixed with sweat, leather, and smoke. Servants and guards huddled near the flames, their laughter sharp, their words cutting. They seemed almost eager for the spectacle inside. I edged close enough to warm my hands, but my eyes kept searching for Jesus. Through the doorway I caught glimpses—priests surrounding Him, accusations flying, guards jeering. They spit in His face, blindfolded Him, and struck Him with their fists, taunting Him to prophesy. Each blow struck something deep inside me.

The servant girl at the gate peered closer, the torchlight flickering across my face. Her voice was sharp, certain: "You are not one of His disciples, are you?"

My throat tightened. A thousand answers surged in me, but the words that escaped were a coward's—"No, I don't know Him."

I turned my face toward the fire, as if its glow could burn away the shame. But inside, my thoughts were a storm. I had sworn to Him only hours ago that I would never deny Him, even if it cost me my life. Yet here I was, denying Him at the question of a servant girl.

Another voice rose out of the circle. A man studied me and said with conviction, "You are one of them."

My pulse pounded. Heat rushed through me, not from the fire but from panic. "No, I am not!" I said louder than I intended. Their laughter rippled, but suspicion lingered in their eyes.

I tried to steady myself, but I couldn't silence the sound of their fists striking Him. I couldn't stop staring at His figure inside—silent, enduring, bearing everything they hurled at Him without a word in His own defense.

And then came the third. A servant of the high priest, a relative of the man whose ear I had struck with my sword in the garden, looked hard at me. "Didn't I see you there with Him?" Another added, "Surely you are one of them. Your accent gives you away."

It was as if every eye in the courtyard fixed on me. Fear swallowed me whole. My words came out like venom to protect myself: "I swear to you—I do not know the man!"

The moment the words left my lips, the sound cut the night air—the crowing of a rooster. My knees weakened. And then—He turned. Across the courtyard, bruised and mocked, His eyes found mine.

That look—I will never forget it. Not anger. Not rejection. Just truth. Sorrow. Love so deep it broke me more than any blow could.

My insides collapsed. Everything I had lived for these past years suddenly felt wasted. I had left my nets, my boat, my family to follow Him. I had sworn my loyalty again and again, promising I would stand even if everyone else fell away. And now—I had failed Him in the very moment He needed me most.

The shame was unbearable. My mind screamed that I could have stopped this. I could have drawn my sword again, fought harder in the garden, shielded Him, taken His place. Anything but this—standing in the shadows, watching Him struck and mocked while I saved my own skin with lies.

I stumbled from the courtyard, unable to bear the sight of Him or the sound of my own cowardice echoing in my ears. The night swallowed me whole, and I broke. Sobs tore from me, heavy with regret. I wept because I had let Him down. I wept because the One I loved most was being dragged away, and I had done nothing—worse, I Peter, had denied I even knew Him.

And yet even in that moment, the memory of His eyes held me. No curse, no rejection, only love I could not understand.

Scriptures: Matthew 26:57-75, Mark 14:53-72, Luke 22:54-65, John 18:15-27

30 Pieces of Silver

THE MORNING CARRIED A weight I will never forget. The elders and priests gathered early, their verdict already set—Jesus must die. They bound Him tightly and dragged Him to Pilate, the Roman governor. To them, it seemed they had control. But I could sense there was more happening than their schemes. The air itself felt charged, as if unseen powers pressed in around us.

One of the younger brothers beside me whispered, "James, how do you know all this so clearly?"

"Because I was there," I answered quietly. "I saw it with my own eyes."

Not long after, the one who had betrayed Him stumbled into the temple courts. His face was drained of life, his steps uneven. The coins clinked in his hands, those thirty pieces of silver—the very price placed on the Son of God. With a cry that pierced the stillness, he flung them across the stone floor. 'I have sinned!' he shouted. 'I have betrayed an innocent man!'

The priests glared with cold eyes. 'What is that to us? That's your problem.'

I watched him turn and flee. It was clear—he had given himself over to darkness, and Satan had used him completely. The same voice that lured him to betray now drove him into despair. Later, word reached us that he had hung himself. The deceiver had devoured him and cast him aside.

None of this took Jesus by surprise. Around the table, only hours before, He had told us, 'One of you will betray Me.' The words struck us like a blow. Each of us searched our own soul, asking, 'Is it I, Lord?' But He revealed it plainly—it was the one who dipped bread with Him. Even in that moment, the Master's eyes carried compassion. He gave opportunity for repentance, but hardness won, and Satan entered fully. What Jesus spoke was now unfolding before us, exactly as He had said.

The sound of those coins still rings in my ears, clattering across the temple floor, echoing in that sacred place like thunder. The priests bent to gather them but refused to put them into the treasury, calling it blood money. They who plotted the death of the Innocent pretended to guard holiness. With that silver they bought the potter's field, a place for strangers' graves.

And in this, the words of the prophets came alive. Zechariah had written: "So they counted out for my wages thirty pieces of silver. And the Lord said to me, 'Throw it to the potter'—this magnificent sum at which they valued me!" (Zechariah 11:12–13 NLT). Jeremiah spoke of the purchase of a field with silver, a burial place for the poor and foreigner. Every detail—down to the very use of those coins—was spoken beforehand.

It was then I understood—this was no ordinary betrayal, no random turn of events. This was war. An unseen enemy moved the betrayer, the priests, even Pilate, like pieces on a board. Yet every move only served to fulfill the plan of God. Darkness thought it was gaining victory, but in truth, the Son of God was stepping into His purpose. He was not overtaken—He was offering Himself.

Scriptures: Matthew 27:1-10

The Lamb Before the Priests

(THE JEWISH TRIALS)

I remember the night as if it still lingers in my bones—the flicker of torches, the press of soldiers, the heavy sound of chains binding Him. My Lord, my Teacher, was treated as though He were the most dangerous of men. I followed at a distance, not daring to draw too near, yet unable to turn away.

They led Him first to Annas, the old high priest, still a power among our people. The chamber smelled of damp stone and oil lamps, the air alive with tension. Annas questioned Him about His teaching and His followers, his eyes sharp and probing.

Jesus did not flinch. His voice carried through the hall with steady calm. "Everyone knows what I teach. I have preached regularly in the synagogues and the Temple, where the people gather. I have not spoken in secret" (John 18:20 NLT).

One of the guards, enraged by His courage, struck Him across the face. The sound cracked like a whip. My stomach turned, my hands trembled. Yet Jesus lifted His head and said, "If I said anything wrong, you must prove it. But if I'm speaking the truth, why are you beating Me?" (John 18:23 NLT).

They dragged Him to Caiaphas, where the Sanhedrin had gathered, their robes swishing like predators circling prey. Witness after witness rose, twisting His words, contradicting each other. I wanted to cry out at their lies, but fear pressed my throat shut.

Finally, the high priest himself demanded, "Are You the Messiah, the Son of God?"

Jesus met his gaze. His words were fire and light. "You have said it. And in the future you will see the Son of Man seated in the place of power at God's right hand and coming on the clouds of heaven" (Matthew 26:64 NLT).

Gasps filled the room. Caiaphas tore his robes, shouting, "Blasphemy! What more do we need?" Spittle flew from his lips. And with one voice, the council condemned Him. They spit in His face, struck Him, blindfolded Him, mocking, "Prophesy, Messiah! Who hit You this time?"

I could hardly breathe, my soul crying within me, "How can this be happening?" The One who spoke life, who healed with a word, was mocked and beaten by those entrusted to guard truth.

When dawn broke, weary though they were, they gathered again—the full council, determined to make their verdict official. "Tell us, are You the Messiah?" they demanded.

Jesus replied with calm strength, "If I tell you, you won't believe Me. And if I ask you a question, you won't answer. But from now on the Son of Man will be seated in the place of power at God's right hand" (Luke 22:67-69 NLT).

"So, are You claiming to be the Son of God?" they pressed.

"You say that I am," He answered.

Their verdict was sealed. "Why do we need other witnesses? We ourselves heard Him say it!" And with that, they bound Him again, dragging Him to the Romans.

I remember standing in the shadows of the temple courts, my fists clenched, my mind reeling, grief surging like wildfire, and I was utterly powerless. I was John, the disciple who leaned on His shoulder, who had tasted His love so deeply. And now I watched the leaders of my own people deliver Him to death.

Scriptures: John 18:12-23, Matthew 26:57-68, Luke 22:66-71, Matthew 27:2-14, Luke 23:7-12, Mark 15:6-15

The Lamb Before the Nations

(The Roman Trials)

They brought Him to Pilate, the Roman governor. I moved with the crowd, keeping to the edges, praying somehow this ruler might see what our leaders refused to see.

Pilate studied Jesus, his eyes narrowing. "Are You the king of the Jews?"

"You have said it," Jesus replied (Matthew 27:11 NLT).

The priests swarmed with accusations. "He stirs up rebellion!" "He forbids paying taxes to Caesar!" "He claims to be a king!" But Jesus remained silent. Pilate leaned forward, frustration creasing his brow. "Don't You hear all these charges they are bringing against You?" Yet Jesus gave no reply, and Pilate was amazed.

As Pilate debated, a messenger entered quietly and handed him a note. I saw his eyes flicker as he read. It was from his wife. Later, I learned her words: "Leave that innocent man alone. I suffered through a terrible nightmare about Him last night" (Matthew 27:19 NLT).

Pilate's face darkened with unease. He knew this Man was no criminal. Yet the pressure of the priests bore down on him, their voices sharp with threats. Rome demanded peace in this volatile land, and Pilate's position balanced on a knife's edge.

When he learned Jesus was from Galilee, Pilate saw a way to escape the snare. He sent Him to Herod Antipas, who was in Jerusalem. Herod had long desired to see Jesus, hoping for some sign, some miracle. He questioned Him at length, but Jesus remained silent. The priests shouted their accusations, while Herod and his soldiers mocked Him, dressing Him in a royal robe before sending Him back to Pilate (Luke 23:7-11 NLT).

Pilate tried again. It was the custom at Passover to release a prisoner. He thought surely the crowd would choose Jesus. "Whom do you want me to release to you—Barabbas, the murderer and rebel, or Jesus who is called the Messiah?"

The priests stirred the crowd until their cries shook the courtyard. "Barabbas! Give us Barabbas!"

Pilate raised his hands. "Then what should I do with Jesus, who is called the Messiah?"

"Crucify Him!" came the roar.

"Why? What crime has He committed?" Pilate's voice wavered with desperation.

But the mob only shouted louder, their cries drowning reason. "Crucify Him!"

I saw the struggle on Pilate's face. He knew Jesus was innocent. He wanted to release Him. Yet the priests hissed their threats—if Pilate let this man go, he was no friend of Caesar. The weight of politics, fear, and pride bore down upon him.

Finally, he called for water, washing his hands before the crowd. "I am innocent of this man's blood. The responsibility is yours" (Matthew 27:24 NLT).

The people cried back, "We will take responsibility for His death—we and our children!"

And so, Pilate released Barabbas. He ordered Jesus flogged, His back torn by the Roman whip, and then handed Him over to be crucified (Mark 15:15 NLT).

I stood in the courtyard, my body shaking, tears stinging my eyes. I, John, the disciple whom He loved, saw my Lord condemned by both our leaders and the might of Rome. Yet even in His silence, even in His suffering, there was no fear in Him. Only love. Only resolve. Only the unshakable certainty that what He was enduring was not defeat, but the very path to victory.

Scriptures: John 18:12-23, Matthew 26:57-68, Luke 22:66-71, Matthew 27:2-14, Luke 23:7-12, Mark 15:6-15

It Is Finished!

As they led Him away, my heart sank. The sound of the whip still echoed in my ears, its cruel lashes tearing His back. The Romans used a scourge weighted with bits of bone and lead at the tips. Thirty-nine times they struck Him, each lash ripping deeper into His flesh until His body was torn and blood poured freely. I could hardly bear to watch. His face, once so full of life and light, was swollen and bruised, His form beaten so severely He was nearly unrecognizable.

And then it came back to me—the words of the prophet Isaiah. "But many were amazed when they saw Him. His face was so disfigured He seemed hardly human, and from His appearance, one would scarcely know He was a man" (Isaiah 52:14 NLT). I trembled as the realization sank in: this was what the Scriptures had foretold. The Messiah would bear such violence, such wounds, that even those who loved Him could scarcely recognize Him.

The soldiers took Him inside the governor's headquarters, gathering the whole regiment around Him. They stripped away His clothes and draped a scarlet robe across His torn shoulders. Twisting thorns into a crown, they pressed it onto His head until blood ran down His face. They placed a reed in His hand as a mock scepter and knelt before Him, sneering, "Hail! King of the Jews!"

Their laughter was cruel. They spat upon Him, took the reed from His hand, and struck His head again and again. Each blow made me flinch, yet He did not resist. His silence carried more power than all their mockery. When their twisted sport had run its course, they tore the robe away, put His own garments back on Him, and led Him out to crucify Him.

A man named Simon from Cyrene was forced to carry His cross. Jesus stumbled often, His body too weak to bear the weight. Women from the city followed, their cries breaking through the clamor of soldiers' commands. I watched Him turn to them, bruised and bloody, and still His concern was for them, not Himself: "Daughters of Jerusalem, don't weep for Me, but weep for yourselves and for your children." Even in His agony, He carried the burdens of others.

When we reached Golgotha, the soldiers began their grim work. I could hardly believe my eyes as I looked upon Him. His face was swollen and bruised beyond recognition, His body torn from the scourging, His frame so weakened that each breath seemed a struggle. Yet even in that brokenness, there was no resistance in Him.

They did not have to force Him onto the cross. I saw it with my own eyes—He stretched Himself out willingly. With quiet resolve, He lay down upon the rough beam, His arms extended, His feet positioned where they would be fastened. It was as though He was embracing what He came to do, offering Himself as the Lamb for the altar.

The soldiers moved with cold efficiency. One placed a long, iron nail against His wrist. Another raised the hammer high into the air. My stomach churned, my legs trembled, and I wanted to cry out, "Stop!" but no sound left my lips. The hammer fell with a sickening crack of metal striking metal, and the nail tore through flesh into wood. Jesus' body jolted with the force, yet He did not resist.

They moved to the other arm, pressing it against the wood. Again the hammer rose, again the iron pierced through His flesh. Each blow echoed in my ears like thunder, searing through my soul. Finally, they bent His knees and crossed His feet, placing one nail through them both. The sound of the hammer striking against the iron spike was unbearable. His blood darkened the wood as it flowed freely.

I cannot begin to comprehend the pain. The nerves in the hands and feet are the most sensitive, and the weight of His body would soon pull against those wounds with every breath. Yet He endured it all, willingly. He did not thrash against them, did not curse, did not cry out in rage. He gave Himself.

As they lifted the cross upright and let it drop into its place, the jolt shook His torn body violently. I winced at the sound, but His eyes—oh, His eyes—still held a depth of love and purpose that pierced through my despair. In that moment, I knew beyond all doubt: this was no accident, no loss of control. He was choosing this. He was laying down His life for us.

Above His head they placed a sign, written in three languages, declaring the charge against Him: "Jesus of Nazareth, the King of the Jews." Some mocked the title, others were offended, but to me it was truth written for all the world to see.

Two criminals were crucified beside Him, one on His right and one on His left. The crowd jeered, the rulers scoffed, and the soldiers mocked, saying, "If You are the King of the Jews, save Yourself!" Even one of the criminals hurled insults, but the other rebuked him, crying out, "We deserve to die for our crimes, but this man hasn't done anything wrong. Jesus, remember me when You come into Your Kingdom." Jesus turned His battered face toward him and spoke with a voice steady and full of promise: "I assure you, today you will be with Me in paradise."

As the hours passed, darkness covered the land from noon until three in the afternoon. The sun itself seemed to hide. I stood near His cross with His mother, her sister, Mary the wife of Clopas, and Mary Magdalene. Their sobs rose and fell with the wind. Some of the other women who had followed Him from Galilee were there also, faces streaked with tears, hands clasped together in anguish. They had served Him, walked with Him, and believed Him to be the One. Now they watched helplessly as His life was drained away before their eyes.

The weight of sorrow pressed down on us, yet His gaze found us in the shadows. With trembling lips He said, "Dear woman, here is your son." And to me, "Here is your mother." From that moment on, I John, took her into my home, carrying His trust as though it were the most sacred treasure.

The ground shook, and the air grew heavy as His time drew near. His parched lips whispered, "I am thirsty." They lifted a sponge soaked in sour wine to His mouth. He received it, then lifted His voice one last time, crying out, "It is finished!" and "Father, I entrust My spirit into Your hands!" His head fell, and the very earth groaned as if it too felt the tearing of creation.

The earth shook, rocks split open, and tombs broke wide. The curtain in the Temple was torn in two from top to bottom. Even hardened soldiers trembled. One centurion, staring at Jesus, said with awe, "Surely this man was the Son of God!" His words pierced me. A Roman, the very hand of His execution, recognized what so many of our own leaders had refused to see.

I looked around at the faces in the crowd. Some stood stunned and silent, others wept openly, beating their chests in grief. A few slipped away in shame, unsettled and afraid. Yet others still muttered in anger, their hearts unchanged. But for me, the cross had unveiled it all. The Lamb of God had been slain, the innocent for the guilty, love poured out for the world.

Scriptures: Matthew 27:32-56, Mark 15:21-41, Luke 23:26-49, John 19:16-37

Nicodemus: The Disciple

THE SUN WAS SETTING, and the Sabbath was drawing near. My heart was heavy, weighed down by grief, yet something within me had shifted forever. For too long I had followed Jesus from the shadows, afraid of the council I belonged to, bound by my position and my fear of losing reputation. But the cross stripped all hesitation from me. After seeing Him give His last breath, I knew I could never again remain silent.

Joseph of Arimathea, a good and righteous man who had not consented to the council's decision, moved with courage and went to Pilate himself to ask for the body of Jesus. My steps fell in beside his. I could not let him bear this alone. My silence had been loud enough already.

We carried with us spices and ointments. I brought seventy-five pounds of myrrh and aloes, more than enough for a king. That was the truth—He was our King. Not just Israel's, but the world's. My hands trembled as I laid down the costly gift, remembering the night years earlier when I had come to Him under the cover of darkness. He had spoken then of being born again, of the Spirit moving like the wind. I hadn't understood fully, but tonight His words burned like fire inside me.

Together Joseph and I took down the body. The Roman soldiers had done their brutal work—His back torn from the lash, His hands and feet pierced by iron nails, His side opened where the spear had entered. My eyes stung with tears, but we worked gently, carefully. With every touch I felt both grief and reverence. This was no ordinary burial. This was love being honored, prophecy being fulfilled before our eyes. Isaiah had written of Him being with a rich man in His death. And here we were, Joseph's own new tomb waiting in a nearby garden.

As we wrapped Him in linen with the spices, the fragrance rising around us, another revelation pressed into my spirit. The sacrifice offered on that cross was not just the surrender of one day, but the culmination of thirty-three years. Every step, every word, every breath He lived was holy. He had never sinned—not once. If He had, even once, He would have been disqualified as the spotless Lamb. But here before me lay the only man who had ever walked this earth blameless, the true Lamb of God without blemish, offered for the sins of the world. His entire life was the preparation for this moment.

We laid Him in Joseph's tomb. The stone was rolled across the entrance, heavy and final. The women who had followed Jesus watched nearby—Mary Magdalene, Mary the mother of Joseph, and others. Their sorrow was deep, yet their love kept them near, unwilling to leave Him even in death.

As the last light faded from the sky, I stood in silence. My fear was gone. I no longer cared who among the Pharisees whispered my name, or what judgment they hurled against me. The cross had broken me, but it had also remade me. I was no longer a secret disciple, but a bold follower.

I remembered His words from that night long ago: "For God loved the world so much that he gave his one and only Son, so that everyone who believes in him will not perish but have eternal life" (John 3:16 NLT). I had seen the giving. I had seen the Son lifted up. And though I did not yet see clearly how life would come from this death, I believed.

So I left the garden that night with a heart torn yet resolute. The old Nicodemus—the one who came by night—was buried with Him. What would rise, I could not yet imagine. But I knew this: my life would forever testify that Jesus was, and is, the Messiah, the Son of the living God.

Scriptures: Matthew 27:57-61, Mark 15:42-47, Luke 23:50-56, and John 19:38-42

The Church Age

33 AD and Beyond

Mary Magdalene

I STILL REMEMBER THE days when darkness ruled me. My mind was a prison, my body weary from battles I could not win. Seven demons tormented me, twisting my thoughts, leaving me restless and broken. People turned away, ashamed of me or afraid of me. I was the woman no one wanted near. Hope felt like a word for others, not for me.

Then He came. Jesus.

He looked at me, and His gaze didn't turn away like everyone else's did. His eyes were steady, full of a love I had never seen. With just a word, He commanded the torment to leave me. In a moment, the chains shattered, the voices fled, and peace poured in. It was like the first sunrise after a stormy night—the kind of light that fills every shadow.

From that day, I followed Him. I couldn't stay away. Alongside other women, I helped provide for Him and His disciples as they traveled. I listened to His teaching, each word like living water to my soul. I saw Him touch lepers no one else would touch, lift children into His arms, forgive sinners others wanted to stone. He gave me back my life, and in return, I gave Him my heart, my devotion, my everything.

That is why the cross broke me. I was there when they nailed Him down, when the hammer struck the spikes that pierced His hands and feet. I stood near His mother and the others as He hung there, His blood soaking the ground. My Lord, the one who set me free, was dying before my eyes. When He breathed His last and cried out, "It is finished," it felt as though my life had ended too.

I followed Joseph of Arimathea and Nicodemus as they laid Him in the tomb. I saw the stone rolled across the entrance. I stayed, unwilling to leave Him behind, until the guards made us go.

The next day, the religious leaders went to Pilate. They remembered that Jesus had said He would rise after three days, and they were afraid of His disciples stealing His body. Pilate gave orders for soldiers to secure the tomb. They sealed the stone and stood watch, thinking they could stop what God had already planned.

The Sabbath passed in silence, but my soul burned with grief.

When the first light of dawn broke on the first day of the week, I couldn't wait any longer. Along with the other women, I carried spices to honor Him. As we walked, we wondered who would roll away the heavy stone. But when we arrived, the earth shook beneath us. The stone was already rolled back, the guards trembling on the ground like lifeless men.

An angel stood before us, his face shining like lightning, his robe dazzling white. My knees buckled at the sight. He said, "Don't be afraid! I know you are looking for Jesus, who was crucified. He isn't here! He is risen from the dead, just as He said would happen. Come, see where His body was lying. And now, go quickly and tell His disciples that He has risen from the dead" (Matthew 28:5-7 NLT).

We looked inside. The tomb was empty—only the strips of linen remained. A storm of awe and wonder tore through me. Could it be true? Could He be alive?

We ran to tell the disciples. Peter and John raced back to the tomb with me. John reached it first, Peter right behind. They saw what I had seen—the linen wrappings lying there. Then they went back, but I stayed. I couldn't move. I stood outside weeping, the ache in me too deep for words.

Through my tears, I looked inside again and saw two angels sitting where His body had been. They asked me why I was crying.

"Because they have taken away my Lord," I said, "and I don't know where they have put Him."

Turning, I saw a man behind me. I thought He was the gardener. He asked, "Who are you looking for?"

"Sir," I begged, "if you have taken Him away, tell me where you have put Him, and I will go and get Him."

Then He said my name. Just one word. "Mary."

Everything inside me leapt. That voice—I knew that voice. My tears turned to joy as I cried out, "Rabboni!" Teacher. Savior. Lord.

I fell before Him, but He told me not to cling to Him. Instead, He gave me a mission: "Go find my brothers, and tell them, 'I am

ascending to my Father and your Father, to my God and your God'"
(John 20:17 NLT).

I ran with joy flooding my soul, the same way peace had flooded me the day He set me free. My voice carried the greatest truth
the world had ever heard: "I have seen the Lord!"

Later, word spread of the guards going into the city. They told
the chief priests what had happened. The leaders gave them a large
bribe, instructing them to say the disciples had stolen the body
while they slept. Even then, they tried to cover the truth. But I
knew. I had seen Him with my own eyes.

The One who had broken the chains of demons in me had now
broken the chains of death itself. I, Mary Magdalene—the woman
once lost in darkness—was the first to see the Light of the world
risen. And I will never stop telling His story.

**Scriptures: Matthew 27:62-66, Matthew 28:1-15, Mark
16:1-11, Luke 24:1-12, John 20;1-18**

Emmaus

I HAD WALKED THE road from Jerusalem to Emmaus many times. Seven miles of dust and stone, winding through hills I knew by heart—the olive trees, the dry air clinging in the throat, the scent of earth warmed by the sun. Often it was just a road home, but that day it carried the weight of sorrow with every step.

The sounds of the city still echoed in my ears—the cries of the crowd, the hammer striking nails, the final words of a dying man. I had seen Him, our Teacher, our Hope, lifted on a cross. I had watched His body lowered, wrapped in burial cloth, sealed in the tomb. With Him, all our hope had been buried. The dust under my sandals seemed to press it deeper into me. The only words I could find were these: "We had hoped."

Our voices were low, heavy, as we spoke along the way. The taste of grief was bitter in my mouth. The road that had always felt familiar now seemed endless, each mile stretching beneath the weight of despair.

Then came the sound of another set of footsteps. A man approached and began walking beside us. His presence was steady, strangely comforting, though His face was not one I recognized.

He asked gently, "What are you discussing so intently as you walk along?"

We stopped, the sadness plain on our faces. "You must be the only one in Jerusalem who hasn't heard," I said, my voice trembling. We poured out our sorrow—the story of Jesus of Nazareth, a prophet powerful in word and deed, the betrayal by our leaders, His crucifixion. And the strange, confusing reports from the women that very morning: the empty tomb, angels declaring He was alive. We told Him everything, yet still we did not see.

Then He spoke. His voice carried weight, yet was laced with compassion. "You foolish people. So slow to believe all that the prophets said. Wasn't it clearly predicted that the Messiah would have to suffer all these things before entering His glory?"

And as we walked, He began to explain. From Moses through the prophets, He unfolded the Scriptures as though every page had always pointed to Him. His words poured over us like cool water on parched lips. My heart stirred, then burned, as if a fire had been kindled deep within me. Along those seven miles, the hours themselves seemed to fall away—time stood still. The road, the hills, even the ache of sorrow faded until there was nothing left but His voice. Steady. Alive. Eternal. Each word lit flame upon flame inside us until our hearts blazed.

By the time we reached Emmaus, the sun was sinking, painting the hills with shadows of gold and purple. The cool of evening settled in, carrying the smell of smoke from village fires. He made as if to go on, but we could not let Him leave. "Stay with us," we pleaded. "It is nearly evening—the day is almost gone."

Inside, lamplight filled the room, shadows flickering against the walls. We sat at the table, a simple loaf of bread before us. The air felt thick, as if holding its breath. He reached for the bread, lifted His eyes, blessed it, and broke it.

The sound of the bread splitting was sharp in the silence. Its fragrance filled the room, warm and familiar. In that moment, our eyes were opened. Recognition surged like lightning—this was no stranger. This was Jesus. Alive. Risen. Sitting at our table.

Overcome, my heart hammered within me, tears filled my eyes as hope, once buried, now burst into flame. Before a word could leave my lips, He was gone.

The silence was alive with His presence. We turned to one another, trembling. "Didn't our hearts burn within us as He walked with us on the road and explained the Scriptures?"

The bread still lay broken on the table, but everything had changed. We could not sit still. Though the night was dark, though the road was long, our feet flew across it. Seven miles we had trudged in despair, we now ran with joy too fierce to hold in. The cool night air stung our faces, our lungs burned, but our hearts soared.

Bursting into the room where the eleven and the others were gathered, we cried out with fire in our voices: "The Lord has really risen! We have seen Him!"

The road that had begun with dust and sorrow ended in revelation and flame. What we thought was the end had become the beginning—and my heart still burns with the presence of the risen Savior who walked beside us.

Scriptures: Luke 24:13–34

Fishing

THAT NIGHT ON THE Sea of Galilee, the water was calm, but inside me was anything but peace. My mind could not escape all that had happened—the cross, the burial, the empty tomb, and the risen Lord standing before us in the upper room. Everything I thought I knew had been shattered. I had imagined a throne, a kingdom, a place at His side. Instead, I had found myself swearing I never even knew Him. Three times. That shame clung to me like chains I could not break.

I went back to what I knew—fishing. But the nets stayed empty all night. Every time I dragged them up with nothing inside, the same question rose in me: Why am I even out here? Who am I now? What am I supposed to do?

Then at dawn, a voice called from the shore. "Fellows, have you caught any fish?"

"No," we replied.

"Throw out your net on the right-hand side of the boat, and you'll get some!"

And in an instant, memory flooded me. Another empty night. Another miraculous catch. Another call: "Don't be afraid. From now on you'll be fishing for people."

The nets filled to bursting, yet not a single thread tore. I knew. I knew it was Him! John whispered what my soul already cried: "It's the Lord!"

I didn't wait. I pulled on my tunic, leapt into the water, and swam to Him. And when I reached the shore, there was a fire—charcoal glowing, fish cooking, bread waiting. The sight of that fire pierced me. I remembered another fire, where my lips had betrayed Him. Three denials by the glow of coals.

We ate in silence, the crackle of the fire the only sound. His hands served us bread and fish, just as He had on that night before the cross. A fire stirred within me when His gaze fell on me.

"Simon son of John, do you love me more than these?"

The question cut straight through me. I felt His heart in it—not harsh, not condemning, but searching. He wanted more than words. He wanted the truth of my heart. And I wanted to give it. "Yes, Lord," I said quickly, almost desperately, "you know I love you."

A faint warmth flickered in His eyes. "Then feed my lambs."

Silence hung for a moment. I thought perhaps it was enough, but then He asked again.

"Simon son of John, do you love me?"

The words pressed deeper. I saw the sorrow in His eyes—the sorrow of the night I had denied Him, the sorrow of the wounds still visible in His hands. Yet I also saw longing there, a longing to restore what had been broken. "Yes, Lord," I said again, my voice softer now, more pleading, "you know I love you."

His gaze didn't waver. "Then take care of my sheep."

And then, after another pause, the third question came.

"Simon son of John, do you love me?"

It broke me. My throat closed, my eyes burned. It was as though every denial I had spoken was being brought into the light, one by one. Three times I had denied Him; three times He now asked for my love. I felt the weight of my own failure, but also the weight of His mercy. He wasn't wounding me—He was healing me. Yet the pain of it tore at my soul.

"Lord," I whispered, my voice trembling, "you know everything. You know that I love you."

And with a tenderness that wrapped around every wound inside me, He said, "Then feed my sheep."

Each question was not condemnation—it was restoration. For every denial, a confession. For every wound, a word of healing. For every failure, a new calling.

Then He spoke of my future—that when I was old, my hands would be stretched out and I would be led where I did not want to go. He spoke of my death, a death that would glorify God. And then, just as He had at the very beginning by these same waters, He said, "Follow me."

In His eyes I saw no anger, no disappointment—only love, fierce and unshakable. He had not only forgiven me; He had entrusted me again with His sheep, His people, His mission.

The fire, the questions, the pain—it all led to this: His heart reaching for mine, and mine finally laid bare before Him. He had restored me. He had called me again.

And His words still burn in my soul: "Follow me."

Scriptures: John 21:1-25

From Nets to Nations

I CAN HARDLY PUT words to what we lived through in those days. The One we followed, the One we saw beaten, crucified, and buried—He stood alive in front of us. None of us could have imagined such a moment.

That evening we locked ourselves away, fear choking the room. The same rulers who demanded His death could come for us at any moment. Suddenly, without warning, He was there—Jesus. His voice was like steady fire as He said, "Peace be with you." He showed us His hands and His side, the wounds still raw, and joy exploded inside me. I had walked with Him from the shores of Galilee, but now I was standing before the risen Son of God.

He breathed on us and said, "Receive the Holy Spirit." It felt like the very breath of heaven filled my being. Then He spoke of forgiveness—of us being sent into the world as the Father had sent Him. It was too much for my mind to grasp, yet my soul burned. This was no longer about following a teacher; He was commissioning us to carry His life into the nations.

Eight days later, Thomas was with us. He had resisted, saying he would never believe unless he touched the wounds. Jesus came again, the same sudden presence filling the room. He looked straight at Thomas, inviting him to place his hand in His side. I'll never forget the moment Thomas fell to his knees, his voice breaking: "My Lord and my God!" None of us doubted after that.

Then in Galilee, on the mountain where He had told us to meet Him, He appeared again. We dropped to our knees in worship, though some still wrestled with the wonder of it. His words pierced us deeper than anything I had ever heard: "I have been given all authority in heaven and on earth. Therefore, go and make disciples of all the nations, baptizing them in the name of the Father and the Son and the Holy Spirit. Teach these new disciples to obey all the commands I have given you. And be sure of this—I am with you always, even to the end of the age."

The world itself seemed to shift as He spoke. What we had just witnessed—the cross, the empty tomb, His very presence alive before us—was not the end of His story. It was the beginning of ours. He was entrusting us with His mission. Not just to tell people about Him, but to make disciples, to raise up followers who would live by His words and walk in His ways.

Later in Jerusalem, He opened the Scriptures to us. For the first time, I could see it—every line from Moses, the prophets, the psalms—all of it pointing to Him. Repentance and forgiveness weren't just ideas anymore; they were the heartbeat of heaven being poured into the earth, beginning in Jerusalem and flowing outward to the nations.

Then after 40 days of breaking open the scriptures, teaching, and imparting Truth, we walked with Him to Bethany. There, He lifted His scarred hands over us and blessed us. As He did, He began to rise—lifted from the ground until a cloud took Him from our sight. My knees nearly gave way. Those same hands that had healed the sick and broken bread for the crowds, those same hands nailed to a cross, were now raised in blessing as He returned to the Father.

We stood there stunned, the air heavy with awe. Yet in that silence, something had changed. We weren't the same fearful fishermen who once dropped our nets to follow Him. We were witnesses—called, commissioned, and forever marked by His presence.

We returned to Jerusalem filled with a joy that no prison, no enemy, no persecution could ever steal. Day after day, we worshiped in the temple. The words of His promise rang through me—He is with us always. And so, as we go, we make disciples. Not because we are strong, but because He is alive.

Scriptures: Matthew: 28:16-20, Mark 16:12-20, Luke 24:35-53, John 20:19-29

Epilogue

To know Jesus is to love Him — and to love Him is to be forever changed. As His presence fills our lives, He draws us into the greatest calling of all: to love the Lord with everything we are, and to let that love overflow into the way we treat those around us. Knowing Jesus is not only about personal devotion; it is about reflecting His heart in how we live, speak, forgive, and serve.

Every step of this journey points us back to what matters most. It is not about striving, achieving, or proving ourselves. It is about walking in relationship with Him, hearing His voice, and letting His love shape our lives. The more we know Him, the more we will live out the very words He spoke — words that bring our faith into action and turn knowledge into love.

> "Jesus replied, 'You must love the Lord your God with all your heart, all your soul, and all your mind. This is the first and greatest commandment. A second is equally important: Love your neighbor as yourself.'"
>
> Matthew 22:37-39, NLT

About the author

Tim Sawtelle

Tim Sawtelle's life has been a journey of creativity and leadership, driven by a passion for helping others grow into their full potential—whether in technology, aviation, ministry, live video production, or education.

As a software engineer, Tim designed and programmed robotic equipment, diving deep into problem-solving and innovation. Later, he became an air traffic controller at a major Air Route Traffic Control Center (ARTCC), helping control and support the safe operations of over 2.1 million aircraft each year—including military, commercial, and general aviation flights (and even working Air Force One a few times).

Tim eventually moved into full-time ministry, serving as a video director at a large multi-campus church, where he built volunteer teams and created training resources to equip others. He also taught live production courses as an adjunct professor at The King's University, sharing his experience with worship and media students. A teacher at heart, Tim has a genuine love for encouraging others to grow in their gifts.

Now retired, he enjoys peaceful writing days and has published several books—with more still on the way. He lives in Arkansas with his wife, Sherri, where they look forward to their country drives, sweet family time, and the joy of grandparent life.

Learn more at:

timsawtelle.com and greenmountainjourney.com

Also by Tim Sawtelle

Jesus Unveiled is part of a larger journey. God has been showing me that His presence isn't just something we read about in Scripture—it's something to live and experience every day. Each of my books reflects that truth in different ways: some offer practical guidance, others bring encouragement, and some provide tools to help create spaces where people can encounter Him.

If *Jesus Unveiled* has stirred your heart, these other books may meet you in different seasons of life and faith.

To get updates on new releases – more books coming soon:

Sign up at my website timsawtelle.com

You can also follow me as an author on Amazon—just head to amazon.com, search "Tim Sawtelle," and click follow.

Sherri and I also share a ministry website filled with stories, resources, and encouragement about walking with Jesus:

More at greenmountainjourney.com

If you enjoyed this book, I'd be grateful if you left a review on Amazon or wherever you purchased it. Your words help others considering this book hear your perspective and decide if it might speak to them too.

Life Unveiled
By Tim Sawtelle

If life came with a manual, it would look a lot like *Life Unveiled.* This is the book everyone wishes they had when first stepping into the unknowns of real life—full of big decisions, unexpected turns, and lessons best learned with wisdom, not regret. Though written with young adults in mind, it's a resource for anyone at any age who wants guidance and wisdom from God's perspective on the many areas of life.

Packed with faith, encouragement, and real-world advice, *Life Unveiled* helps you navigate money, work, relationships, and purpose with confidence and clarity. From writing a résumé to managing your finances, from dating with intention to building a family, from planning your future to learning the value of rest, every topic goes deeper than surface tips—equipping you to make wise choices, build a life that lasts, and walk with God every step of the way.

Real life doesn't require perfection—just faith, wisdom, and the courage to take the next right step.

Pick up your copy at timsawtelle.com or amazon.com

Hope Unveiled
By Tim Sawtelle

Embark on a remarkable journey alongside Tim Sawtelle as he shares events from his life in *"Hope Unveiled: Stories of God's Unwavering Faithfulness."* This captivating book chronicles Tim's life, a amazing testament to God's steadfast presence through every twist and turn, through moments of triumph and adversity.

Discover a narrative woven with the threads of Tim's experiences, where the journey of faith meets the embrace of the most faithful Father. Through these compelling stories, witness the profound ways God revealed Himself, transforming Tim's life and illuminating the path with hope even in the darkest hours.

Join Tim on his quest for meaning, purpose, and truth, as he unveils the intimate relationship he experienced with the greatest Father of all—God. *"Hope Unveiled"* invites you into the heartwarming journey of one man's life, a testament to the enduring faithfulness and the unending love of a Father who never lets go.

Pick up your copy at timsawtelle.com or amazon.com

Stewarding the Atmosphere
By Brandon D. Marx and Tim Sawtelle

Unlock the full potential of your ministry by investing in your most valuable asset: your people. Equipping them with advanced video and lighting techniques and a healthy team dynamic will have a profound impact on your ministry.

Stewarding The Atmosphere is crafted for pastors, worship leaders, college students, technicians, and volunteers, offering innovative strategies to elevate your visual experience and cultivate an atmosphere that truly connects people with God.

Pick up your copy at timsawtelle.com or amazon.com

www.ingramcontent.com/pod-product-compliance
Lightning Source LLC
Chambersburg PA
CBHW060410130626
46555CB00005B/2023